Published by QuestVersity

The World's Easiest Book label is owned by QuestVersity

Visit our website at www.questversity.com

First published in 2021

Some of the characters and events portrayed in the stories found in this book are fictitious. Any similarity to real persons, living or dead, is coincidental and not intended by the author.

ISBN: 978-0-578-25801-0

Printed in the United States of America

The World's Easiest Book on Becoming Antiracist:

Strategies for Countering Racism in the 21st Century

Dr. DuBois Teddy McMillan

Other Books and Courses by Dr. DuBois Teddy McMillan

FICTION
(under Teddy McMillan)

Diamond Lane: A Fleetwood Mahone Story

Sol & Simonton

NON-FICTION

The World's Easiest Mini-Book on Improving your Memory Using Memory Palaces (late Fall 2021)

Five Eleven and a Half: A Nappy Headed Kid from Compton (coming in Spring 2022)

COURSES/CONSULTING

The World's Easiest Course on Becoming Antiracist
- see our website for more information on courses and consulting services

Dedication

To everyone who saw something wrong with the color-coded system of inequity and sought to change it, so that we might bring people together and live better lives. I'm eternally grateful and indebted to the countless examples of human sacrifice to discover humanity's greatest asset, the one thing that links us all and capable of conquering our greatest obstacles, and that's *love*.

To my mother and father, you inspired me and groomed me to who I am today. To this day, I find my deepest sense of pride when saying, "I'm Gip and DuBois' baby boy."

To my big sister, my biggest cheerleader and fan, your baby brother finally finished that project that I told you about. I miss you dearly, Sadi. I feel your presence though I cannot see that big smile and cute chuckle, "Look at my brother! He wrote another book," you would probably say. I'll see you again one day. I love you.

To my Queen and my three sensational children. You've witnessed my daily struggles with this project. There were ups and downs, and more downs. But, you inspired me throughout the process. I would not have completed it without you. I love you dearly.

To my brothers and sisters. I thank God for your love and guidance over the years. I've shared some of our experiences in this book to let people know just how important you are in my life. I love you.

To my former and present students. I must apologize for not going as hard as I wished to disrupt power systems that affected our lives. As with the journey of life, I'm still learning. I did my best, but my best-best is yet to come. It is my hope that this book informs you and inspires you in some way.

To my former teachers and coaches, you didn't let me take the easy way out. You challenged me in ways that helped me develop resilience, and through these experiences, I've shaped my voice and purpose.

Table of Contents

Introduction

At some point in my life, I learned that I'm Black. I knew it was not the same type of "black" found in the assortment of colors in a crayon box, or the dreaded bitter-tasting black licorice or black jelly beans that never got chosen and left at the bottom of candy packaging or crystal bowls sitting on top of an antique tea table. It wasn't the superstitious black cat that we were told to not let cross our paths or we would surely be doomed. The black I'm talking about had to do with the way I look, the way I talk, where I live, the music I listen to, the food I eat, the people I come in contact with the most, the kinkiness of my hair (the hair I used to have), and the life experiences that shaped me because someone or something classified me as "Black" and treated me a certain way because of this labeling. It's the experiences that are my motivation for writing this book. I wanted to know why things are the way they are. Why are outcomes in various areas of human activity predictable along color lines? I needed to explore some fundamental questions about color and race. I wanted to know where it came from? Who created it? How was it created? When was it created? And the most powerful question: Why was it created? I hope that many of these questions are answered throughout this book. I've created several activities that will help you think and reflect on experiences and apply core values to life-like scenarios.

This book and approach are probably quite different from what you are used to. Let me say this now, I'm a visual-kinesthetic learner. I prefer images, pictures, and hands-on experiences -- that's how I learn. As a kid, I found myself sketching concept maps on paper while my teacher delivered a lesson. I carried this on to college, and when I sat in a boring lecture hall and had to watch a professor stand at a podium and speak to us for an hour, I found myself using the same strategies I had used throughout my educational career. I began doodling and would sketch images and figures of the key elements in the lecture and tie them to something hilarious. For instance, if the teacher/professor was lecturing on the branches of government and separation of powers, I would likely create three vertical columns and draw pictures inside of each one related to the type of power held in that branch. For the President, maybe I would sketch a muscular figure with a huge "V" on the character's toe. Of course, the President has the "power" to "veto" laws. I didn't wait for the teacher/professor to draw this on the board; I had developed a natural tendency to do it myself. I bring this up because I know many learners are visual or kinesthetic learners and don't get many opportunities to learn in a way they prefer. Some studies suggest that up to 65% of us are visual learners.

I developed this book to appeal to all types of learners and various age groups. You will find that it feels more like an experience or a workbook than a history book. It's not a history book. I once heard someone say, "People don't read history books." Well, I don't think this is true. I love history and read some books for leisure and others for research. Some books capture my attention better than others. What I've found that works best for me is, the books that keep me most interested are written using basic language. I like them because they remind me of Mrs. Morgan, my 6th-grade teacher, or one of my brothers or sisters who taught me so much about life, or my parents, aunts, or uncles. For example, my oldest brother once taught me how Volkswagen engines work. He used to build them in his garage from scratch with no manual. It was exciting to sit there watching him carefully place small parts into the engine block. After he turned the wrench slowly and came to stop, he would lean forward and squint his eyes to ensure the connection was tight while I watched on. "Okay, it's your turn now," he mumbled, with a hint of excitement in his tone. After I had my try at it, he asked questions about what I had just done. I answered to the best of my ability then he would discuss technical terms with me. That would typically conclude with a trip to a parts store where I would hear the language of engine building between him and the store owner and gain a deeper understanding of the process. That is an example of a proven learning model called **experiential learning**. I'll continue with the story. After purchasing new parts, this would likely spark a conversation on our way home, where he cleared up any confusion I might have on the process. With this new information, I would be prepared to connect it to a new experience such as my brother asking me to connect the same part to another engine. We will use a similar method in this book. I want you to draw in this book, take notes, and sketch funny images if you have to.

First, race is a touchy topic. The form of racism that I am addressing in this book is a color-coded brand of racism. It was formed in early colonial history in America, and I will cover it in-depth throughout the book. I break racism into five categories or layers, and I dedicate a chapter to each one using an experiential learning model. Each chapter opens with a story. We will reflect on the story, connect with personal experiences, learn about the topic, and apply core principles to a new experience. In Chapter 1, I introduce you to the concept of racism. The goal here is for us to come up with a clear definition of racism to ground the work. In Chapter 2, we explore the ideological framework that shaped the belief that some groups are innately inferior to others, thus, creating a premise for justifying the enslavement of human beings. In Chapter 3, we explore how ideology informs the structures that make up our social world. Moving from the structures and the systemic nature of racism, we take a look at racism at the institutional level in Chapter

4. In this chapter, we uncover inequity in the school system and think of ways to address it. In Chapter 5, we explore cultural norms, beliefs, and conduits of messaging such as the media that perpetuate stereotypes. The last category is the interpersonal layer, and we cover this in Chapter 6. Interpersonal racism is also called person-to-person racism and it might come in the form of hate speech, violence, or anything that can cause hurt or harm to another person due to their racial group membership. In the last chapter (Chapter 7), we apply everything that we have learned throughout the book, apply it to two scenarios, and create a plan to address potential inequities.

Examining race is a complex endeavor. The goal of this book is to help us understand it and apply strategies to disrupt it when we see it operating. I have listed several sources throughout the book that I encourage you to explore to learn more about it.

I think America will realize its best days when racism no longer exists. I have faith that we are moving in that direction.

Please visit our website at **www.questversity.com** for more activities, videos, and resources for this book. Again, this is not just a book. This is an experience.

Chapter 1
What is Racism?

Racism is a socio-politically constructed system of inequity.

The purpose of this chapter is to help you become familiar with race and explore how racism was used to create divisions amongst people based on the color of one's skin.

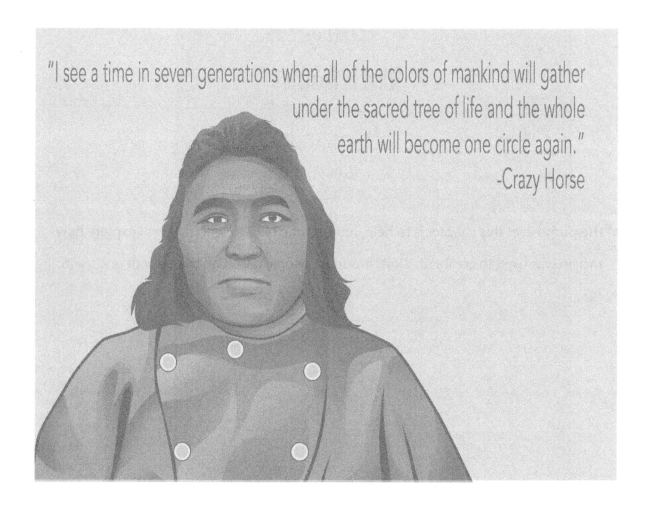

"I see a time in seven generations when all of the colors of mankind will gather under the sacred tree of life and the whole earth will become one circle again."
-Crazy Horse

...what you will be able to do at the end of this chapter:

- understand what is meant by "race"
- construct your own definition of race
- understand what racism is and learn how it was/is used to create divisions amongst people
- create a mockup of an infographic that informs others about racism
- understand the TREC (*think-respect-empathy-compassion*) Method and how it can be used to address inequities

...materials needed for this chapter:

- construction paper (poster board or printer paper also work)
- colored markers (various colors)
- scissors
- tape
- access to the Internet

Of all the issues facing humanity, racism has probably caused more destruction than anything else over the last 400 years.

Racism and other forms of oppression have a long, rooted history in America from the very conception of this country. While the struggle for freedom has proven to be long and enduring, what is even more complex is the notion of universal freedom and the processes that must be implemented to reconcile centuries of power imbalances that have shaped our society. As an African American, reared in an era where the struggle for civil rights appeared to be a thing of the past, there were many instances that forced me to think critically about freedom and what it meant to be truly liberated. As much as one would like to believe that enslavement is limited to physical bondage, true freedom requires deeper analysis and cannot be defined in one "all-encompassing definition".[1] To even begin the conversation, we must take a look at race and what it means in this country. Racism is a form of oppression, though not the only one. To become anti-racist, we must first have a common understanding on what it is before we can identify it. If not, it would be difficult to address it. But, this isn't easy. It's highly elusive, but what's contained in this book are proven strategies to unlock our collective power to disrupt its course. Each chapter ahead takes an in-depth analysis of each layer of racism with exercises to help equip you with the knowledge and skills necessary to apply to real-life experiences.

In this chapter, we will be learning about race, look at how others have defined it, reflect on a personal experience, and engage in an interactive scenario where you will have an opportunity to apply your knowledge in a lifelike simulation using the TREC Method. The goal is for you to develop a clear definition of race and racism, which will set the groundwork for understanding what we mean when we say we are becoming anti-racist on our job, in our homes, our communities, our nation, and our world. Read the story on the next page.

"Racism is the father of race."

Ta-Nehisi Coates

I wrap my hands tightly around the grip area of the solid 29-inch wooden bat and raise the bat just over my right shoulder and begin a slight circular motion, preparing for my older brother Terrance to wind up and release the pug ball. We had made it out of an old t-shirt, aluminum foil, and masking tape. Our driveway is narrow and if I hit the ball to straight center field, I know I have enough power to send the ball over the sidewalk on the other side of the street to get a home run, and that would surely end the game. We might even make it inside the house before the streetlights come on. Though our parents haven't set such serious restrictions on us as some of our friends' parents, it's just doesn't make much sense for us to play pug ball in the dark. Terrance finally winds up and releases a pitch right down the middle. I dip my front shoulder and raise my front leg, coil like a spinning top, and unload on the ball with a crushing swing. The ball takes flight and rips through the tree clear across the street.

"You got that one," Terrance yells, while turning and watching the ball land flat in our neighbor's driveway and dribble a few feet more just short of their gate.

"I'll get it," I say, darting past Terrance and panning my head to spot cars moving down the street. No cars. I pick up the ball and meet Terrance back in our driveway as he's picking up our gloves and the cardboard square used as our only base.

"You getting stronger. Just keep hitting that ball," he says, pushing his lips back to form an slight smile. "We gotta hurry up, that new movie coming on tonight."

"Which one?" I ask, squinting to express my curiosity.

"It's called Roots."

***

I've always known I'm Black. There has always been a deep, soulful energy around being black that I can't quite explain in words. It's something to be proud of, it's beautiful, and it's also something you bear, almost like carrying a heavy boulder up a steep hill. The weight can become overbearing, taxing, exhausting, but you can't give up because struggle is a part of who we are.

As Terrance and I enter the house, clean up and grab some of our mother's delicious Sunday cooking, I feel a tingling in my stomach and excitement rushing through my mind as we prop pillows and lay blankets on the floor of our modest three bedroom house in Compton, CA, for a family night of entertainment watching our floor model television set. Our daddy fixes TVs and he tells us Zenith is the best.

"What's the movie about?" I ask Terrance, who is getting the TV ready. He keeps his focus on the channel knob, turning the tuning dial and maneuvering the antenna to straighten the scrambled picture.

"It's about slavery."

"Sla-ve-ry?" I mumble, in a long, monotone voice.

"Yeah, you know. When white people put us in slavery." A bedroom door creaks open.

"Terrance and Teddy, what time that movie come on?" My sister Sonja yells from her room door.

"It's about to come on in a few minutes," Terrance says. The door to our den opens, and another brother moves into the kitchen and swings the door of the refrigerator open.

"I'm 'bout to make some popcorn," Bert says. He cuts off a chunk of butter from a long cube and flicks it into a hot skillet, and the butter bubbles and sizzles away. "Y'all want some?"

"Yeah. We want some."

"Make me some too, Bert," Valarie yells from the living room.

"Whassup, dude?" My big brother Jeff enters the living room and squats on the arm of the couch.

"We about to watch Roots," I beam in excitement. "I'm 'bout to make some Kool-Aid," I say, scooting off of the couch and darting into the kitchen. I reach into the freezer and pull out two blue ice trays, slam the trays onto the counter and watch *the cubes pop up.*

"Make some for everybody," Valarie says.

We dim the lights and get comfortable around the television set.

My mother comes out of her room and settles on the couch. "Whatchall watching?" she asks.

"It's a movie about slavery," I say. "They gon' show how white people came to Africa and took us away."

"Oh, I heard about this movie," Mama says.

"Mama, did that really happen?" I ask.

"Yeah. Them old folks back home be saying they came and took us away from Africa and brought us here and put us in them fields picking cotton and working for white folks."

The crunchy texture and salty taste of popcorn chased with the tangy burst of Kool-Aid is simply euphoria for a seven-year-old kid. I snuggle between my siblings, anxious to see the unfolding of my past.

I immediately connect with Kunta Kinte and relate to the complex family structure of the Mandinka tribe, which is quite similar to my own family dynamic that extends back to Alabama. I see myself in Kunte, the boy warrior trying to make sense of the world around him as he transitions into manhood. His grandmother (played by Maya Angelou) reminds me of my grandmother, Big Lula. His mother (played by Cicely Tyson) is caring and nurturing like my mother. His father is tall and strong, like my father. Kunta is introduced to men in his community, just like I'm cared for and looked after by my brothers, uncles, cousins, and men in my community.

Kunta's world is completely disrupted, turned inside out, and transformed from warrior to chattel, human to beast, and I'm crushed.

1. What can you infer about the relationship between Terrance and Teddy? List two things.

2. When Teddy said he connected with Kunta Kinte, what does this mean?

3. Why do you think Teddy says, "I am crushed"? Explain.

4. Describe your own personal experience when you first learned about race or racism?

5. Define the following in your own words:

Race:

Racism:

Next, read the **Teddy & Terrance** story in **visual form**. This will prepare you for the next activity.

Activity #2: My First Experience with Race/Racism (Story Strip)

In this activity, you will be recalling the very first time you were made aware of/or experienced race or racism. It can be a personal experience, something you heard or saw through some form of media, or an experience that someone else had with race or racism that you may know.

Draw or sketch the story below using the panels provided. You can be as elaborate as you want or you can make it simple by drawing stick figures or faces. Use as many or as few of the panels as you need. Be sure to include speech bubbles in your panels. Use the Story Strip on the previous pages as a reference. Feel free to split the panels in halves. I want you to put some thought into this activity.

Story Title:

Activity #3: Share your Story (Group or Individual)

Share your story with a partner. If you are taking the class online and working independently, please feel free to share your story with a family member or a friend. Use the questions below as a guide. After sharing your story, ask them the following questions. Listen to their responses without interrupting them or casting judgment. It's important that you simply listen and jot down notes.

1. How do you think this event has affected my life? For clarity: After sharing your story, "you" are asking someone this question about "your" life.

2. Are there similarities in my first experience with race or racism and yours? In what ways? In what ways are they different? Again, you are asking this question to someone you shared your story with.

What's the BIG THING ABOUT Race?

As we explore race and take a deep look into the system of racism, it is important that we first come up with a clear definition of race and racism so that we can work on becoming *anti-racist*. Now, I know it might feel a bit uncomfortable exploring this topic, and it might even create some level of anxiety and discomfort, but we must dig into how it has been used to dehumanize groups of people based on racial classification.

In general terms, think of **race** as a way in which people have been grouped based on the skin color. Now, that wasn't so bad, right? As I'm writing this section, I'm reflecting on a former student I had when I first started teaching in the mid-1990s. There was a street war going on in Compton over the death of Tupac Shakur and students often came to me to gain some perspective. I vividly remember the student bringing up the Rodney King incident in the same conversation and asking the question, "What's the big thing about race?" I have pondered and grappled with this question for a long time, and still do to this day. I have spent countless hours conducting research, reading books, going to lectures, and experiencing "race" firsthand through the lens of a Black male growing up in Southern California. I've come to understand race as a critical influencer in my entire life experience. It influenced where I lived, how much money my family had, where I went to school, what resources were available to me, and my overall life trajectory. Much of the literature on "race" will suggest that it is a social construct. We have all heard or read about inequities (or injustices) living in our social world and how some people are discriminated against due to slight differences in how we are made up, whether these markers (characteristics) consist of skin color, ethnicity, culture, or group membership. We are going a little deeper in this book.

"Think of social construction as something that has been created by people and accepted through some social understanding."

First, let's think about what is meant by a "social construct". Whenever terms like this are used, it's important for us to break them down into easy-to-understand terms so that we can really understand what they mean. Think of social construction as something that has been created by people and accepted through some social understanding or social agreement, whether we are aware that we are involved in this agreement or not. Something as simple as the use of profanity is socially accepted and constructed as "inappropriate behavior". So, in essence, we have agreed that the use of profanity isn't showing good behavior. These beliefs are likely reinforced at home, at school, while riding the public bus, while shopping in stores, etc. Still with me?

Here's another example, the dollar bill is simply a piece of paper with green and black ink, artistic designs, symbols, and a former president on the front. Without a socially constructed meaning, this piece of paper would be meaningless and worthless. As a society, we have come to establish meaning to what a one dollar bill means, a twenty dollar bill, and so on. Each piece of paper has its own value based on some agreed upon term and is used as a means for exchanging goods and services. This isn't limited to American currency; this example can also be applied to other mediums of exchange such as the Yen, Euro, and Cryptocurrency. But, back to the dollar. Think of how there isn't much of a difference in the design of $1 bill, $5 bill, $20 bill, and the $100 bill. What is the main difference in these bills? The value, right?

> "Race has been limited to categorizing people based on skin color."

Race was constructed in a similar way. Throughout history, we have read about groups of people being taken into captivity as a result of conquest or war. But, 15th Century conquests to lands outside of Europe spurred a new way of using power to separate, dehumanize, and classify people based on skin color. We will touch on this in the next chapter on **Ideological Racism**.

So, the important takeaway is that we understand that race has been limited to categorizing people based on skin color and using this single trait to make broad generalizations about people, and constructing a power system to oppress and dehumanize people who have been classified in one of the "non-white" racial classes such as black, brown, red, or yellow. These broad generalizations about one's skin color are then transformed into socio-political constructs where beliefs about one's race is reinforced and practiced through a system of inequity.

For a long time, I totally agreed with this definition, but in recent times, I've come to understand that calling it a "socially" constructed thing doesn't account for the legal or political meanings that influence and shape experiences. It also leaves a door open to critique and judge cultural norms against the group in power. For instance, when I apply for a job or apply to renew my driver's license, they ask for my race. This act is a legal claim. They are not asking how I see myself "socially"; they give me options that have been pre-determined based on some criteria. Dorothy Roberts includes the legal aspect of race in her definition. She believes race is a "political system that governs people by sorting them into social groupings based on invented biological demarcations."[2] As evidence, we will see how "white" was constructed in the 1600s in Virginia by legal definition. In his work, Theodore Allen, another renowned researcher, asserted that there had never been, on any documents in the history of America, a group of people called "white" until the 1600s.[3]

Jacqueline Battalora supports this claim when she said, "in spite of the common experience of 'race', we should begin by realizing that 'white' people, as a designation of a group of humanity, much less as a race, never existed until late in the seventeenth century".[4] We will explore this more in the next two chapters as we take a look at a critical point in this country's history when a rebellion triggered laws to be passed that resulted in the creation of the race that we now call "white".

> "White people... as a designation of a group of humanity... never existed until the late seventeenth century."
>
> - Jacqueline Battalora

Answer the questions below in a small group, or you can also work on them individually if you are working alone. There are no right or wrong answers to these questions. Answer them as honestly as you can.

1. Does your original definition of race differ from what was just presented in this section?

2. Highlight or underline Dorothy Roberts' definition of race. Why do you think she calls it a political system?

3. Based on what you already know about race, how was/is it used?

Which Came First, Race or Racism?

One of the first things that's important for us wrap our brains around is that racism, as we have defined it, is a purposeful system of inequity that was created to justify the enslavement of African people, the annihilation of Indigenous people of this country, and the marginalization of people from Mexico and Asia. When we think of it as a "system" of oppression, we see the motivation to carry out these acts come before the intentional and deliberate classification of people based on skin color. As Ta-Nehisi Coates puts it, "race is the child of racism; not the father."[5] Using biblical references, philosophy from Greek writers from the past, and claiming legal authority, the Portuguese used the combination of these sources as reason to justify the enslavement of people from the western coast of Africa in the early 1400s.[6] Angela DiAngelo, author of the popular book *White Fragility*, supports this claim when she wrote, "the idea of racial inferiority was created to justify unequal treatment; belief in racial inferiority is not what triggered unequal treatment."[7] To put it in simple terms, racism came before race. Thorough coverage of this will take place in the next two chapters.

Why Study Racism? My Early Teaching Days

The students' din was a mixture of footsteps, books flopping on desks, and the hissing sounds of "shhh", as students eased back into the classroom after an extended break on a hot spring day. They were eager to start a conversation on race and I was anxious to demonstrate how deeply seeded racism is in our subconscious and how powerful perception is in shaping our beliefs, and how we then generalize these beliefs onto a whole group of people. Before break, one student had started the conversation by blurting out "all White people are racist", though we weren't discussing race, and I'm not sure as to why this statement was even made. Something triggered her and I thought it was a good opportunity to at least show her how we might look deeper into the "system" of racism, and not the individual players that may hurt or harm us in some way. It was only a few weeks before that a student shared his personal perspective on the American classic, To Kill a Mockingbird. He felt it was totally senseless for us to read the novel because, he said, "it ain't got nothing to do with us", he mumbled, soon after I placed the book on the edge of his desk, excited to explore one of my favorite stories with a new group of students. Sharing this student's uneasiness about reading the book only to give you some context as to the type of open conversations I had with students. My goal in starting a conversation around the young lady's statement about "all White people" being racist was to get students to think about what race really is. Though I had only been in the profession for a few years, I felt confident enough that I would be able to shift their thinking a bit using a scenario that might help clarify some things. I didn't believe "all White people are racist", and I still don't to this day. But, I understood where the student was coming from. Working in an alternative school setting, many of my students had already formed ideas and drawn conclusions based on their personal interactions with a system that had historically mistreated Black and Brown people. In complete transparency, I felt the system had also mistreated me.

Let's give the student the name Claudine. In my 27 years in education I don't think I have had a single student with this name, so it's safe to use. Claudine sat at her desk with her chin resting peacefully in her palms with her elbows planted well on the table, bouncing her leg up and down and anxious to get started. As the other students settled down, I moved to the board and wrote a large "T". On one side of the "T", I wrote down these four roles that we might find in a business: president, accountant, secretary, and director of operations/security. You might think, why would you need security? Well, stay with me for a moment. On the other side of the "T", I wrote the following: Asian, Black, Hispanic, and White. I then asked students to match the job titles on the left with a person on the right. So, do you see what I'm getting at? Overwhelmingly, students selected the White person as president, Latino person as secretary, Asian person as accountant and the Black person as director of operations/security.

If hearing all of my students selecting exactly the same thing wasn't convincing, I then asked them this: "Where would I be?". After ten to fifteen seconds of complete laughter, the majority said, "You would be the head of security." Now, I have absolutely nothing against the role of head of security, but this is telling for an entire group to place you in a category based on your racial identity. To take it a step farther, I've been on the campus of a school that I've worked for on nights where parents were present and have been asked, "Are you the director of security?" On these two occasions, they were shocked that I was an assistant principal.

I shared this story to get us to think about the psychological effects of racism and how they play out in our minds and also in society. Racism functions in many forms. In this book, we will analyze racism through a multi-layered lens, so that we can address it when we see it operating. Looking back on my conversation with students, what I didn't know at the time was how "ideology" and "culture" were feeding and informing personal beliefs. That's why we'll examine racism in layers.

Layers of Racism

We will analyze the different layers of racism throughout this book. The aim is for us to know how to identify where racism is operating and address it by creating a plan and taking action. As we have already established, and based on what you may already know, racism is an extremely complex system with several moving parts. Many times, we see racism played out on television or on some social media platform, we might hear about experiences through others, or perhaps we might see it unfold right before our eyes. No matter where it's coming from, it's important for us to know *how it is situated and how it is operating.* What I mean by this is, which layer is it coming from? Knowing where it is operating plays into how we address it. For instance, if there is a policy in an institution like a school where the same teacher is constantly writing referrals on the same group of students because they are not "acting right", this might be causing an inequity and denying children an opportunity for equal access to the curriculum. Though the discipline matrix might not have any blatant discriminatory wording against a particular group, the enforcement of such policy might be having a disparaging impact on a specific group of students. So, if we are only viewing this through an institutional or structural lens, we might not see how the lack of cultural understanding might be playing out in these spaces. In addition, if there is no understanding of how ideology has gone into shaping perception, we would likely not see how telling a child they "aren't acting right" can be disrespectful or flat out dehumanizing. What is "acting right"? Who determines that? Where did that come from? Based on whose standards? These are the type of basic questions we must ask in order to get to the source of the problem. This can also be applied to the work world where a specific group is denied employment or certain cultural characteristics are viewed in a negative light.

In each of the next five chapters, we will explore the five layers of racism. I am not professing to know everything about racism and these five layers are not something that are set in stone. You can do a Google search and see that other writers and researchers have created their own frameworks for examining racism. I've found these five layers to make the most sense for simplifying a complex system by breaking them into five manageable parts. I've tried to make each chapter easy to follow with activities to spark critical thinking, constructive dialogue, personal reflection, and guides on how to identify racism and take action. One of the approaches that my wife and I created while working on our Social Emotional Learning curriculum is called the TREC *(think-respect-empathy-compassion)* Method. We will use this method throughout the book as a tool to help you prepare and take action in life-like scenarios using relevant case studies. There are times when you will be asked to insert dialogue into scenes in order to bring a sense of realism to the experience. I have found this to be an effective way to increase learner engagement. In the next section, I will introduce you to the TREC Method.

Using the TREC Method

The TREC Method is a valuable tool used for constructive and intentional conversation centered on respecting one's humanity, showing empathy, and applying compassion to a problem.

- **Think** - First, you will *think* about the problem. This entails identifying what is happening in the scenario and identifying the problem or issue. For our case studies, we want to be thinking about: *In which layer is racism operating in this scenario?*

- **Respect** - Here, you will make the decision to *respect* those involved in the scenario. Any time we are working towards better understanding and getting ourselves and others to a better place, it's important that everyone's humanity is recognized and valued.

- **Empathy** - As we are working through each of the scenarios, we want to be aware of the opinions of others and their perspectives. Showing *empathy* means that you intentionally shift perspective and place yourself in someone else's situation.

- **Compassion** - Finally, we take a step in the direction of actually helping someone. When we show *compassion,* we are taking action. We will use this step to discuss the "what" and "how" you will help solve the problem.

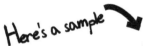
Here's a sample

A Sample of the TREC Method

Using the TREC method to address the dilemma
THINK: What should Mr. Garner be thinking about?
RESPECT: How can Mr. Garner ensure he shows respect as he tries to address the problem?
EMPATHY: How can Mr. Garner demonstrate empathy for the driver in this dilemma?
COMPASSION: What are some ways in which Mr. Garner might show compassion by helping the driver?

How My Art Teacher Used the TREC Method in 1981

There was really no TREC Method in 1981. I just chuckled a bit when I wrote the title for this section. As mentioned, this is something my wife and I created recently as a way to pull from various experiences where adults use language, empathy, and compassion to help us get through tough situations in our lives. There seemed to be a method to the process when listening to dilemmas and providing valuable insight and direction. The whole concept centers on caring and wanting to help another person work through a problem. I was fortunate to have many adults in my life such as parents, relatives, teachers, and coaches, who have employed these strategies in various ways.

Based on what I shared with you at the beginning of this chapter when I first saw *Roots*, I was traumatized. It was a real thing that I just couldn't wrap my brain around. I kept asking the question in my head, "How could they treat other people so badly?" What I didn't know at the time, is that racism, being one of the most cruel acts against humanity, was justified in the minds of those who created the system. I happened to have a wonderful family who was supportive and ensured that they nurtured me, but I really didn't understand how to deal with the brutality that I saw in the movie until my junior high school teacher showed the video to us during class. When I exited the classroom one afternoon, he asked, "So, did you like the movie?" Here is a snippet of that conversation.

Talking to Mr. Davis ⟶

MY CONVO WITH MR. DAVIS

Over the next few weeks, Mr. Davis checked on me to clear up any misunderstandings about the movie. He demonstrated his compassion by listening to me and not judging me for my ignorance of racism. He continued to relate my experiences to his own, as he was a kid growing up during a time of legalized segregation. Listening to his stories gave me mixed feelings of fear and hope. One statement that he made still lingers in my mind after several decades and resonates clearly. He said, "It's a system, son. It's not just about what people do, it's a system." Thank you Mr. Davis. Learning what this "system" is has become a part of my life's journey.

To illustrate the TREC Method, I'll take the position of Mr. Davis. So, if he was completing the TREC Guide below, this is probably how he might have filled it out:

Using the TREC method to address the dilemma

THINK:	Student is confused about what he saw in a movie. All layers of racism are operating.
RESPECT:	I need to understand that he's young and might not understand what he saw.
EMPATHY:	I need to see this through his lens by shifting my perspective.
COMPASSION:	I must be able to offer some help so that we can resolve this issue.

If you pay close attention to the conversation between me and Mr. Davis, you'll notice that he went through each stage of the TREC Method. First, he listened to my initial comment about "how crazy" the events in the movie were and "being confused". He replied with a statement that confirmed he was listening to me, but immediately shifts to a positive outcome from the experience. He wasn't judgmental and concludes his next comment with "I'm glad we're talking about this." This is certainly a sign of respect. He then continues by shifting his perspective (*empathy*) and expressing how he wanted to help me. Though this is a simplistic example of how we will be using the TREC Method, it's a great guide to help us engage in meaningful conversations around daily dilemmas that we face. You will be completing the TREC Guide throughout this book and applying it to like-like scenarios. As we move through the first three steps of the TREC Method (*think-respect-empathy*) and enter the last step, *compassion*, we want to see how we can apply some of the concepts of allyship in this step. As compassion is really about "helping", utilizing these concepts in this phase can result in pretty amazing moves to address injustices.

Allyship

Allyship is an active practice where an individual or group of individuals undertake a role to provide education, activism, and advocacy alongside an individual or community of individuals who have been marginalized in some way.[8] Being an ally is a choice and those who step into a role do so with the intention of working by the side or behind the group or community that has been dis-empowered, never in the front or in the lead. Being an ally does not mean that a person needs to be visible or out in the open about their support. You can also work behind the scenes in many capacities to assist in disrupting the power source that is harming others. In order to create workplaces and communities that are diverse and inclusive, having allies is a critical element in bringing awareness to issues that impact marginalized groups.

When becoming an ally, it is important to understand the identity and experiences of others, understand how the imbalance of power works to marginalize others, and decide to stand in solidarity with the individual or group, while elevating the voice of those who are typically silenced. Once an ally, we can assist in challenging beliefs and call out practices that harm others.

To reiterate how an ally is expected to position herself or himself with an individual or group, we must understand the importance that we must not look to take the lead. We are there in a support role, so we work on the side or behind the cause.

According to the Oregon Coalition Against Domestic and Sexual Violence, here are a few ways to practice allyship:

- Be good at listening to the struggles of others and don't be judgmental
- Respect lived experience. The experts on any form of oppression are the people most directly affected by it, and their analysis of that oppression always takes precedence over the opinions of people who don't experience it.
- Provide unconditional solidarity. That means no "I'd be on your side if you didn't act so angry" (e.g.). You don't get to decide when someone is being too emotional, too rash, too mean, or otherwise "undeserving of your support." Your allyship is not a favor that you can retract when someone responds to their oppression in a way you don't like. You just have to be there.[9]

You will be applying some of these concepts in a case study in the next chapter.

To end this chapter, complete the End of Chapter Checkup and the Project. These activities were created to help you think about the work needed to bring about positive change in our world.

CHAPTER 1 CHECKUP

In this activity, you will be constructing your own personal definition of **Race** and **Racism.** If you are in a group setting, you are encouraged to break into groups of two to four and answer the two questions below after discussing it with one another. If you are working alone, that's fine. Simply answer the questions independently.

- What is your definition of Race?

- What is your definition of Racism?

In this activity, you will given an interactive scenario and where you will be prompted to work through a storyline on racism. At specific points in the story you will have to refer back to what you have learned in this chapter. Don't worry if some things are not clear right now, you will become more familiar with them as we go through the course. Please go to our website and you'll see the link to *Scenario: Chapter 1* under the book's title.

Dilemma

INFOGRAPHIC MOCK-UP

Project: Infographic Mock-Up

Time: 45 minutes

Delivery: Groups of 3 to 4. If you are taking the class online or at
                home, you can work on this independently.

INSTRUCTIONS:
In this project, you are going to be working with a group of 3 to 4 team members. You are tasked with creating an infographic that will be used to help inform your staff, a friend, a family member, or colleague on the meaning of racism.

You should be as creative as possible when designing and developing your infographic, but you do not have to create a digital logo at this time.

Use the materials below to create a mock-up for your logo. You will share your mock-up design with the class at the end of this activity. In later chapters, you will have time to develop your idea into a digital logo.

MATERIALS:
• Poster paper
• Makers
• Pencils
• Scissors
• Tape

When completed, please feel free to upload it post on our website. There is a section on the website called "Post Infographics" where you can post your work for others to see. This is not a requirement. Have fun.

www.questversity.com

Endnotes

1   Hanes Walton Jr. and Robert C. Smith, *American Politics and the African American Quest for Universal Freedom* (New Jersey: Pearson, 2015), 2.

2   Dorothy Roberts, *Fatal Invention: How Science, Politics, and Big Business Re-Create Race in the Twenty-First Century* (New York: The New Press, 2011), 4.

3   Theodore Allen, *The Invention of the White Race, vol. 1, Racial Oppression and Social Control* (New York: Verso, 2012).

4   Jacqueline Battalora, *Birth of a White Nation* (Houston, TX: Strategic Book Publishing, 2013), 1.

5   Ta-Nehisi Coates, *Between the World and Me* (New York: One World, 2015), 7.

6   A.C. DE C.M. Saunders, *A Social History of Black Slaves and Freedmen in Portugal 1441-1555* (New York: Cambridge University Press), 4-46.

7   Robin DiAngelo, *White Fragility* (Boston, MA: Beacon Press), 4.

8   Cornell F. Woodson, "Developing our Ally Identity." PDF file. Accessed on August 16, 2021. https://cpb-us-e1.wpmucdn.com/blogs.cornell.edu/dist/3/6098/files/2016/01/ally-identity-okl2qw.pdf

9   "Working Definition of Allyship," Oregon Coalition Against Domestic & Sexual Violence, accessed August 1, 2021, https://www.ocadsv.org/sites/default/files/resource_pub/allyshipdefinition_handout.pdf

Chapter 2
Ideological Racism

A racist belief system that attempts to justify and rationalize racist actions.

The purpose of this chapter is to introduce you to ideological racism, discuss its origin, and explore how this belief system was formed in Portugal in the 1440s to rationalize the enslavement of people from West Africa and the eventual conquering of Native Americans.

...what you will be able to do at the end of this chapter:

- understand how ideological racism was formed and used to enslave West Africans and conquer Native Americans
- construct your own definition of ideological racism
- analyze information and discuss the impact ideological racism had in Europe and other parts of the world
- discuss how racist ideology has been used in the U.S.
- devise a plan after identifying ideological racism with the goal of

...materials needed for this chapter:

- access to the Internet

Bogus scientific studies

Biological Differences

Religious beliefs

Philosophical beliefs

Racial Hierarchy

Unproven Theories

Cultural Differences

Ideological Racism

Since race is a socio-political system, the group in power has a lot of influence on how a particular race is viewed.

Introduction: Ideological Racism

When we think about an ideology, we typically think about ideas or beliefs that people share. In the basic sense of the word, ideology is a collective set of thoughts and opinions shared by a group of people or an individual that characterizes a certain thing. Ideologies can serve to help us understand the world better and also work to create a systematic way of organizing the collective thoughts and beliefs of people. Sociologists have used ideologies to refer to broad views, beliefs, and basic ways of thinking about particular things in our complex world. On the surface, ideologies aren't bad. When we associate ideology with the categorization of people based on the color of skin pigmentation, it creates a natural division between people and ranks them according to skin color.

In this chapter, we will be exploring ideological racism through a short story, where you will start thinking about how it operates and plays out. You will then reflect, think, and apply your knowledge in a life-like simulation using the TREC Method. The goal is for you to develop a clear understanding of ideological racism, which is a key layer in understanding the other layers of racism that are informed by ideology.

"Slavery was a sophisticated system of oppression that was backed by beliefs..."

■ ■ ■

Abeni raised her hand to shield the sun's harsh glare. She stood with her shoulders straight, her chin tilted up enough to allow her eyes to settle on the bright, blue ocean as she gazed on the waves crashing against the white

sand, and then dribbled back into the vast sea with a hissing sound. This was a typical day. Besides her duty to cast the net into the shallow depths of the ocean to catch fish, she and her fellow female villagers were excited about the annual celebration that would take place later that day. The day was also special because it was the first time Abeni's younger sister joined her on the traditional fishing excursion with other women from her village. Abeni couldn't wait, she felt tingling in her stomach every time she thought about all the fun she would have. "Get the other end," yelled an elderly woman in a raspy tone.

"Okay. I got it," Abeni said, gripping the end of the net and jerking it down with both hands to flatten the center. Several other young women moved in, steadied their feet, and grabbed the ends of the net. "Come right here, Soni," Abeni directed her sister, "you have to hold it right here." Soni grabbed the lining with a muffled giggle.

The elderly woman stood on the small pier that they had made a few years before. "Now, come up here ladies. You have to throw it out far. You can't be worried, just throw it out while someone holds the rope." The women hurled the net and it landed flat, several feet away and disappeared into the ocean.

"Pull now," the elderly woman yells. Abeni, Soni, and other women pulled hard on *the rope.*

"You feel that?" Abeni grunted, wrinkles forming on her forehead as she tugged on the rope.

"We got some fish," Soni yelled with excitement.

When they finally pulled the net from the ocean, they had captured seventeen fish. "This was a great first cast. Let's do one more," the elderly lady said.

The women put twenty-seven fish into the bucket. They laughed and cheered. It was a great day.

As they started back to the village, Abeni caught a glimpse of a boat in the distance. It was one of the boats people had warned them about, with a huge sail at the top and the people on board known to capture people from local villages. "Look." Abeni dropped her bucket and pointed. The women turned back to the ocean. Their faces were taut with fear and their eyes wide.

Within only a few days, the village was raided and many of the people were captured and placed on the bottom of a ship by white men. Abeni and Soni's parents weren't captured and they worried about them. The sisters prayed while the boat traveled across the ocean they had known all of their lives, but had not journeyed. The shackles around Soni's legs were tight and she tried to loosen them, but she didn't have the strength. She cried out to Abeni, who tried her best to comfort her. Abeni didn't know what to think. The choppy ride made her nauseous and she threw up several times. She only hoped they would be set free soon.

After several days, the boat stopped on the shores of Portugal. Abeni, Soni, and others were taken off of the boat. The sun peered down fiercely and they tried to shield its glare. There were moans and cries for help as they were ushered off of the ship and brought to an open area where there were people observing them. Men were saying things that Abeni did not understand. It appeared to Abeni that the men were praying and saying things to honor their God. After a few moments, the captives were separated. Soni cried loudly when she saw Abeni moved forcibly to another group. The two sisters had never been separated in their entire lives. Though some of the people watching on appeared to be angered when seeing the people mistreated and separated, the men continued.

Abeni never saw her sister again. She becamce a servant for a wealthy family and lived the rest of her life in Lisbon, reminiscing on her earlier days as a young child in Guinea.

Activity #1: Discuss in Groups (or as an individual reflection)

1. Describe something unique about Abeni's experience as a girl in Africa.

2. Describe the relationship between the two sisters.

3. What was the response of some of the common people in Portugal?

4. What are you *wondering* after reading this short case study?

Ideological Racism

The foundation of ideological racism centers on the belief that some people are different than others. This "difference" that I'm referring to isn't some trivial difference such as the dye color of one's hair, personality type, or favorite food choice. These differences, in the words of George Fredrickson, "are regarded as innate, indelible, and unchangeable" and associated with one's racial classification based on skin hue or ethnocultural difference.[1] The conquering and enslavement of human beings into perpetual servitude to fuel a well coordinated system for gaining riches, wasn't just some flimsy idea floating around in the heads of a few people. In order to pull off this idea, the Portuguese used various strategies to make their quest "legally and philosophically justifiable" in their minds.[2] They established the belief that West Africans were sinful by nature and "natural" servants.[3] I emphasize the word "natural" here because the sources they used to justify their actions supported the belief that West Africans were born to be slaves, and it wasn't much they could do to change what they were naturally destined to do in life. Though there is a body of research on how many of these same strategies were used against other groups such as Jews and Muslims, I limit my focus to West Africans here to specifically focus on race and the system of racism that flourished in the United States.

When dealing with race, ideology takes on a specific form. Tommie Shelby sees racist ideology as a set of shared beliefs and implicit judgments about people and they are "generally known to be widely held."[4] These distorted views were specifically used against the people of West Africa in the early 1400s (eventually Indigenous people of America, Mexicans, and those from Asian countries) which led to a widespread effort by the Portuguese to capture and subdue many people from

West Africa. Using a racist ideology, the Portuguese developed a narrative that dehumanized people with dark skin, reducing their humanity to savagery to legitimize their quest for dominance by using the institutions of religion, philosophy, and law.[5] We must examine racist ideology and understand how this form of racism contributes to, and continues to inform, other forms of racism that are deeply entrenched in the culture of the United States and threaten our ability to ever truthfully become the "land of the free".

"Racist ideology is a widely held set of loosely associated beliefs and implicit judgments that misrepresent significant social realities."

– Tommie Shelby

Examining Racist Ideology

When we think about racist ideology and start examining some critical moves and events that happened in the past to denigrate people, sometimes these discussions ignite and trigger certain feelings of uneasiness that can cause us to feel angry, upset, vulnerable, mad, helpless, or many other possible emotions. I get that. I've been there and have to also check myself when I delve into this work because it's painful and difficult to process and digest at times. At times I'm just dumbfounded. The layers upon layers of source information don't always lead down the right paths to discovery and help me uncover the exact answers I'm looking for. I often find myself so deeply immersed in the work until I'm either exhausted, or tired of trying to find logic in the complexities of the network of social systems operating non-stop,

24 hours a day, 365 days out of the year. When I examined racist ideology, I narrowed it down to two basic questions:

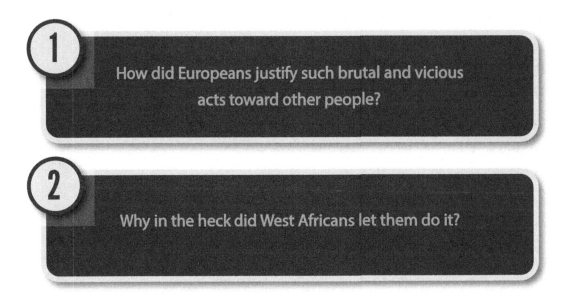

1. How did Europeans justify such brutal and vicious acts toward other people?

2. Why in the heck did West Africans let them do it?

In my quest to find answers to these questions, it's been quite a journey and one that I'm glad to have ventured on, because I've found the most logical answers to these questions to be simple, yet quite disturbing.

This section is not aimed to make anyone feel personally responsible for any of the events that happened in the past that I'm going to share with you. My reason for sharing this information is for us to develop a common understanding of the ideological layer of racism. The goal is for us to better understand how these beliefs were formed, and continue to inform, our structures, institutions, culture, and individuals minds. More importantly, we want to know how to identify it when we see it operating and think of ways to disrupt it.

It is critically important that we open our minds, don't point blame to any person currently living, and don't carry the burden personally for these events. To get the most out of this work, be prepared to engage in constructive dialogue on how we might analyze, reflect, and think of ways to challenge worldviews and beliefs on race. I think this is key to accepting, recognizing, and valuing people, regardless of where they are placed on the racial hierarchy, or any difference about them that is different from what I call the "influencer" culture. I choose to use the word "influencer" rather than "dominant" because there's an implicit tendency to connect words like dominant to superior, and superior to "whiteness". I believe "influencer" culture is more accurate and doesn't make the assumption that being dominant is better, or normal, or right.

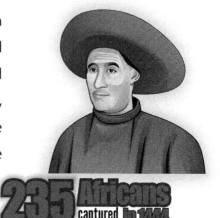

It is safe to say that slavery was a sophisticated system of oppression that was backed by customs, social and cultural norms, and institutions that influenced and guided social behavior. The thought of capturing, enslaving, and forcing people into perpetual bondage and treating them as chattel (property) might seem like a far-fetched idea in modern times, and perhaps was just as unconscionable for the common people, who were enraged when they saw families separated, as documented in the work of Prince Henry's royal chronicler, Gomes de Zurara.[6] Based on the account, there were 235 "Idzagen and black prisoners" captured and brought to Portugal, and once on shore, were taken off of the ships and separated into nine groups.[7] Here, Zurara gets emotional and appeals to God with, "for it is not their religion but their humanity that maketh me weep in pity for their suffering".[8] We will explore this encounter later in the chapter, as you may already see how it was link to the Abeni & Soni story above. For now, let's take a look at **Big Question #1** first, then eventually move on to the second question.

Big Question #1: How did the Europeans justify such brutal and vicious acts towards other people? Let's take a brief look at cognitive dissonance.

Cognitive Dissonance

DEFINITION
cognitive: *thinking, or having to do with thinking*
dissonance: *when things clash, or not having harmony*

As people, we might commit acts that go against some moral code, it might be a personal code or some cultural moral, and as a result, we feel really bad inside. I've done this before when I get angry and something slips out of my mouth like, "Why did you do that? That wasn't the smartest thing to do." Something like this might slide by when you're talking to a teammate, a close friend, or a relative, but what if it's your child, or your parent, spouse, or colleague; it hits a little different. That bit of uneasiness you feel inside might prompt you to apologize, or you might do something else like try to justify why you said it. If I tell someone "that's not the smartest thing to do", I'm essentially saying whatever they did is dumb. When reflecting on my personal belief of being a good person, I can reconcile this by either apologizing to the person, or I might try to justify why I said it by thinking, "well, they deserved it". Though this example is simplistic, it does highlight what we feel when our actions are in direct conflict with how we feel about ourselves.

Here's another example: let's say a person suffers from a certain condition and knows a healthy diet could improve their health but continues to eat junk food. Knowing the behavior is in conflict with what can improve their health and possibly prolong life, but continuing to harm themselves by eating unhealthy food, is called **cognitive dissonance**. Again, there's a conflict between some behaviors, beliefs, or attitude. So, we try to justify the behavior to remove the discomfort that cognitive dissonance brings. Here's an illustration:

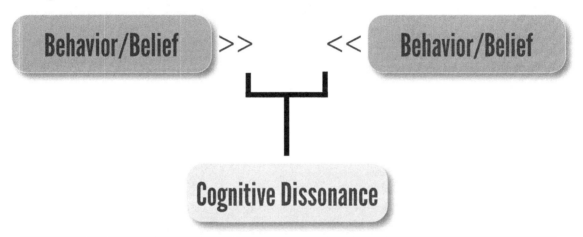

Activity #2: Defining Cognitive Dissonance

In this activity, you will construct your own personal definition of **Cognitive Dissonance**. If you are in a group setting, you are encouraged to break into groups of two to four and answer the two questions below after discussing it with one another. If you are working alone, that's fine. Simply answer the questions independently.

1. Write your own definition of **Cognitive Dissonance**.

Activity #3: Examples of Cognitive Dissonance

In this activity, you will think about other examples of **Cognitive Dissonance** and then write down ways that a belief or behavior might be justified. I gave you two examples above but there are many others. I want you to write down at least three. I give you another example in the table.

	Belief/Behavior	Conflicting Belief/Behavior	Justification/ Resolution
1	Smoking cigarettes is unhealthy	Someone smokes a pack of cigarettes a day	I know people who have smoked longer than I have and they are fine
2			
3			
4			

Shared Beliefs

Think for a moment about all of the thoughts that float around in our brains daily. We essentially take in information through our five senses and the brain goes to work, processing and encoding information through a highly complex neural system consisting of over 100 billion nerve cells and one trillion

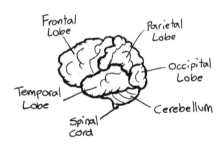

supporting cells. In a recent study published by Newsweek (7/15/20), we have over 6,000 thoughts a day.[9] That's a lot of information to process. While processing, there are certain parts of the brain such as the hippocampus that is responsible for storing information in long-term memory. Short-term memory is limited and can only store information between 20 and 30 seconds, after which it will either be discarded or stored in long-term memory.[10] I bring this up because it's important for us to think about how thoughts help us form ideas on how we interact with our environment, and how these ideas become important in how we function as human beings.

"Our brains process over 6,000 thoughts a day." - Newsweek

"Thoughts help us form ideas on how we interact with our environment."

Check this out. Think about how your life might have been if after touching fire for the first time you didn't learn that fire was hot and maybe you shouldn't touch it again. Maybe it took some of us a second or third time to learn, but hopefully we all got the message, "FIRE IS HOT!" Theorist Jean Piaget first introduced the concept of schema and he believed we constantly change as we interact with our environment.[11] The information that we gather from these experiences is called schema. With the fire example, we typically learn that "fire is hot" after we touch it for the first time. Now, as a baby, we didn't need to understand rapid oxidation and combustion to know, "I shouldn't touch that again." So, schemas serve an important purpose in how we are designed as human beings.

Schema is not limited to an individual, it can also form into "shared" understandings about things. The fire example is one that many of us will be quite familiar with. You might ask, "What does this have to do with ideological racism?" When we think about schemas, they can become powerful because they help us form some common understanding about the world in which we live. According to Sally Hanslanger, they can help us "organize our beliefs in a way that helps us form expectations and process new information".[12] Shared thoughts and meaning help us interact with others and the world around us. When a group shares a schema, it helps members of that group respond to things in a similar way. Based on historical evidence, what initially started as circumstances of war where Africans were forced into slavery upon capture, quickly turned into a lucrative enterprise where ethnocultural and religious differences became the impetus for capture and enslavement. It was through shared schema that racist ideology took root and formed to justify these acts against African people.

The Seeds of Racist Ideology

Prince Henry saw an opportunity to gain financially and he became a key player in orchestrating a system where West Africans were captured and turned into valuable commodities in Portugal and other parts of Europe. Though these acts were considered brutal and dehumanizing, the desire for financial gain and power outweighed guilt, which eventually led to Prince Henry finding ways to legitimize the capture and enslavement of people from West Africa. Saunders claims that Roman and Canon law, the Bible, and the teachings of Aristotle, all had the provisions for slavery and "agreed that the appropriate authorities in any country, Christian or infidel, could reduce prisoners of war and criminals to slavery".[13] Armed with this thinking, Prince Henry forged forward and eventually got backing from the king and the church to capture more West Africans. This was common practice during this era, but wartime capturing of Africans only lasted a "few years in the 1440s".[14] Gomes Eannes de Zurara was one of Portugal's most prized chroniclers, and given the charge from King Affonso V, to "obtain all the information possible" on Prince Henry the Navigator, who was the son of King John I.[15] He sent Portuguese sailors on expeditions down the coast of West Africa, and by 1451, the Portuguese became a maritime power and had mastered ocean navigation and developed a new type of ship called the *caravel*. There are also claims that Henry the Navigator was obsessed with discovering gold and a route to East Africa or India to find a legendary Christian leader by the name of Prestor John. These advancements would place Portugal at the forefront in the Age of Exploration and made them a major player in what eventually became the Trans-Atlantic Slave Trade.

Claims of Bestial Nature

The Portuguese used "otherness" or "differences" to relegate Africans to a bestial and soulless state that made servitude more of a natural destiny rather than one resulting from people being captured during warfare and eventually enslaved. When the Portuguese were able to use their advancements in ocean navigation to cross Cape Bojador and made contact with Africans as far south as Guinea, they captured some of the Africans and brought them back to Portugal on the pretense that they were going to convert them to Christianity. The Africans were isolated and enslaved and said to be "black as Ethiops" and "ugly".[16] Additionally, Zurara noted that the Idzaden and Black Africans captured "had lived in perdition of soul and body; of their souls, in that they were yet pagans; lived like beasts, without any custom of reasonable beings."[17]

> "Prince Henry the Navigator ordered Portuguese sailors on these expeditions and by 1451, the Portuguese had mastered ocean navigation and developed a new type of ship called the caravel."

The capture and enslavement of Africans during this period was a coordinated effort between King Affonso V, Prince Henry the Navigator, and Popes Martin V, Eugene

IV, and Nicholas V. The popes called for support of the Portuguese in their conquest efforts to destroy infidels, and to view the conquest as *crusades* (religious wars) that gave them *plenary indulgence* (frees a person from punishment) for such acts.[18] An **infidel** is a person who either doesn't have a religion or has a religion/belief/spiritual system that is different from someone else's. This opened the gates and gave Prince Henry free reign to capture and subdue Africans to build an economic empire.

Armed with the idea that Africans were bestial in nature, Prince Henry petitioned the church to validate his expeditions as crusades so that he could get their backing and assist them in "Christianizing" the Africans. As a result, bull Illius Qui was issued in 1442 by Pope Eugene IV, giving Prince Henry full remission of sins and declared expeditions down the coast of Africa, crusades.[19] For more in-depth study on this topic, read *A Social History of Black Slaves and Freedmen in Portugal 1441-1555.*

Activity #4: Revisiting Cognitive Dissonance

On your own, please answer the question below. There are no right or wrong answers here. Feel free to reread the section above or conduct research on your own to answer the question.

Describe how the Portuguese handled cognitive dissonance that may have existed with their desire to enslave human beings.

Activity #5: Group Reflection (Wonderings)

Answer the following questions below in small groups of three to four. The purpose of the question is to spark conversation on what we covered. There are no right or wrong answers, but it would be great if the dialogue is centered on what we covered in this section.

1. What are you wondering?

2. How did Prince Henry get backing from the popes?

3. What impact do you think racist ideology had on the common people of Portugal in the early 1400s? (*think about what Zurara documented*)

4. In what ways do you think this ideology influenced early American colonists and eventually the founders of the U.S.?

As mentioned previously, race is a *socio-political system that sorts people based on the color of their skin*, or what Dorothy Roberts calls an "invented biological demarcation". At the end of the Thirty Years' War in Europe (1618-1648), the economy took a huge hit and left a lot of people out of work. To give you some background on the war, it was fought between Catholics and Protestants and one of the bloodiest ever, which resulted in millions of deaths from combat, disease, and famine. The real struggle was to determine which system would prevail and control central Europe.[20] With the hope of finding better opportunities across the Atlantic Ocean in the newly established colonies, many skilled and unskilled European laborers accepted the challenge and came to the newly conquered lands as indentured servants. Twenty African captives arrived in Jamestown, VA, in 1619 on an English warship called *White Lion*. John Rolfe, an English settler who is also known for marrying Pocahontas, documented the landing. Here is an excerpt of Rolfe's writings.

"About the latter end of August, a Dutch man of Warr of the burden of a 160 tunnes arrived at Point-Comfort, the Comandors name Capt Jope, his Pilott for the West Indies one Mr Marmaduke an Englishman. They mett with the Treasurer in the West Indyes, and determined to hold consort shipp hetherward, but in their passage lost one the other. He brought not any thing but 20. and odd Negroes, which the Governor and Cape Marchant bought for victualls (whereof he was in greate need as he pretended) at the best and easyest rates they could. He hadd a lardge and ample Commyssion from his Excellency to range and to take purchase in the West Indyes."[21]

Underline or highlight anything from the excerpt that makes you think about racist ideology, based on what we have covered so far.

1. How does this play into forming racist ideology?

2. Do you think these words are similar to what Gomes de Zurara wrote 199 years prior? Explain.

At the time, there were European and African indentured servants who worked on farms for tobacco landowners. As we will see in the next chapter, there was no group in early colonial history that called themselves "white" at this time.

Indentured Contracts

For European indentured servants, they were sent to the colonies for a set amount of time to work on the land, which was typically three to seven years, and at the end of the period they were freed and able to own land and enjoy the freedoms afforded to other landowners. For Africans who were stolen and brought to the colonies, their plight was different. In many instances they eventually became servants for life. The research suggests that there wasn't much of a difference in how Africans and European indentured servants were treated in general, but indentured contracts shed light on how indentured servants were granted certain rights. Read the words of an actual indentured contract between Wessell Webling and Edward Bennett on the next page.

To all to whom theife presents shall come greeting in o' Lord God everlasting.

Know yee that I Wessell Webling sonne of Nicolas Webling of London Brewer for & in consideration that I have bene furnished & sett out & am to bee transported unto Virginia, at the costs & charges of Edward Bennett of London, marchant & his associates, & for & in consideration that they have promised & covenanted to maintain me with sufficient meat drinke & apparell doe by these presents bind myself an apprentise unto ye said Edward Bennett for the full terme of three yeares to begin the first [fic. feast] of St Michaell the Archangell next after the date of these presents. And I doe promise & bind myself to doe & perform all the said terme of my aprentishippe true & faythfull service in all such labours & busines as the said Edward Bennett or his assignes shall imploy me in, & to bee tractable & obedient as a good servant ought to bee in all such things as shalbe comaunded me by the said Edward Bennett or his Assignes in Virginia, & at the end of the said terme of three yeares the said Edward Bennett do promise to give unto the said apprentice and house & 50 acres of land in Virginia to hold to me my heires & assignes for ever, according to the custome of land there holden, & alsoe shall give to the said apprentice necessary & good apparell, & the sayd apprentice shall inhabitt & dwell uppon the said land, & shall pay yearely for the said fiftye acres of land fro & after the hee shalbe therof possessed unto the said Edward Bennett the yearely rent of 50 shillings starling for ever & two dayes worke yearely, & to all & singuler the covenants aforesaid, one the Party & behalfe of the said apprentice to bee performed & kept in manner & forme as aforesaid. The said apprentice bindeth himselfe to his said Master per these presents: In witnes whereof the Partyes aforesaid to these present Indentures have sett their hands & seales, the 25th of September 1622.

Signett Ed. Bennett
Ext Willm Claybourne[22]

Activity #7: Quick Reflection (Group)

Underline or highlight anything from the excerpt on the previous page that makes you think about racist ideology, based on what we have covered so far.

1. What is Wessell Webling agreeing to do in this contract?

2. What is Webling expecting to get during his journey to Virginia?

3. What is Webling expecting to get at the end of the contract?

4. How do you think this contract benefited the landowner?

5. How do you think the issuance of land benefited the colony?

Things drastically changed when a dispute between a planter by the name of Nathaniel Bacon and the governor of the Virginia colony took place in 1676 that erupted into a full-fledged uprising called Bacon's Rebellion. Bacon had purchased two large estates near the James River. When clashes with nearby Native American groups threatened "territorial expansion", in addition to his desire for vengeance against attacks from the Natives, he appealed to the governor of Virginia, William Berkeley, for swift action.[23] Berkeley's response to the demands didn't satisfy Bacon so he organized a group of indentured servants and enslaved Africans and they clashed with Native groups and eventually made it to the capital of Virginia and burned it down. As a result of the rebellion, strict laws went into place that changed the complexion of indentured servitude in the colonies. According to Dr. Jacqueline Battalora, this is the first time we see the name 'white' associated with any group of people in law.[24] The laws specifically targeted Africans and the brand of slavery that resulted is one of the harshest forms of brutality in known history. We will take a look at the laws in the next chapter when we look at **structural racism**, but for now, we will continue to explore how ideology continued to perpetuate the idea that whites were superior by nature.

18th & 19th Century Racist Ideology

One of the pioneers of racist ideology was a Swedish botanist by the name of Carl Linnaeus. In her seminal work titled, *Post Traumatic Slave Syndrome*, Joy DeGruy highlights some of his claims of differences based on racial classification. While Linnaeus is well known for being the first person for developing a taxonomy of living things which included plants, animals, and humans and much of his work was considered groundbreaking at this time, there were several flaws.[25] First, none of his work was based on scientific evidence. He simply made very broad and inaccurate statements about people, pushing them into these categories based on "skin color."[26] He used more descriptors when working on plants and animals, but when he classified humans, he "used considerably fewer descriptors."[21] Secondly, he added "moral and intellectual" attributes to each of the categories of humans. Again, these assignments were made with little to no evidence whatsoever and served to dehumanize Africans. Linnaeus classified humans by four categories that correlated with geographic areas (*Homo Americanus, Homo Europaeus, Homo Asiaticus, and Homo Afer*). Here is a quick glance on how he depicted each category:[27]

Race	Descriptors
Homo Afer	"black, phlegmatic, cunning, lazy, lustful, careless, and governed by caprice."
Homo Americanus	"reddish, choleric, obstinate, contented, and regulated by customs."
Homo Asiaticus	"Melancholy, stern. Black hair; dark eyes. Strict, haughty, greedy. Covered by loose garments. Ruled by opinion."
Homo Europaeus	"white, fickle, sanguine, blue-eyed, gentle, and governed by law."

Linnaeus' work was accepted as fact and gained broad acceptance as people began to believe this to be accurate descriptors of people along racial lines. There were several other Europeans who added to the body of work that claimed white genetic superiority. We won't delve too much into the topic in this book. For further study of this topic, I highly recommend Joy DeGruy's *Post Traumatic Slavery Syndrome: America's Legacy of Enduring Injury and Healing,* and *Outcasts from Evolution: Scientific Attitudes of Racial Inferiority, 1850 - 1900,* by John S. Haller.

Anti-Black sentiment in Portugal in the early 15th century gave rise to racist ideology. During this era, the justification for the enslavement of Africans was centered more on ethnocultural and religious ideas than a scientific argument.[28] This changed in the 18th and 19th centuries when we see several Europeans from the scientific world attempt to classify humans based solely on skin color. This is dangerous, and as Douglas Fredrickson puts it, these ideas are "proposed to establish a racial order, a permanent group hierarchy that is believed to reflect the laws of nature or decrees of God."[29] So, the impetus for this quest for dominance extended beyond personal or group gain. It was entangled in the belief that perceived biological differences gave a specific group of people the natural right to conquer and subdue others, by viewing it more of a command from a higher source than individual or group desires.

Before we reflect on these classifications and descriptors, read this quote from one of America's most famous figures:

Thomas Jefferson

"I advance it therefore as a suspicion only, that the blacks, whether originally a distinct race, or made distinct by time and circumstances, are inferior to the whites in the endowments both of body and mind."

Activity #9: Racist Ideology Reflection (Group or Individual)

The questions below are for the **Racist Ideology** section. Please work in groups of three to four to answer the questions. Read each question, discuss, then write down your response. If you are working alone, you can simply answer the questions on your own. It is good practice to discuss with someone else to get different perspectives.

1. What were your initial thoughts after viewing the racial classifications by Linnaeus?

2. Have you heard or seen these descriptors played out in the real world? If so, in what ways?

3. Do you see any connection between the work Linnaeus published and the quote by Thomas Jefferson? Explain.

Linnaeus' work laid the foundation for other members of the scientific world to develop racial classifications centered on the same belief that "whites" are genetically superior to other groups. While Linnaneus' taxonomy was centered more on skin color and cultural differences, Johann Friedrich Blumenbach, a 19th Century German physician also known as a race theorist, classified humans in five categories (Caucasian, Mongolian, American, Ethiopian, and Malayan) that considered other features such as skull size, facial characteristics, hair, and color.[30] According to John Haller, Blumenbach considered Caucasians to be the most beautiful of the five groups and "also the basis from which the others derived."[31] Blumenbach's work was accepted as truth and many European researchers who came after him "incorporated" his claims into their work "with little hesitation."[32] This had lasting effects on our world as we see many of these same ideas perpetuated centuries later.

You might ask...what does this have to do with race in the 21st Century? Well, I'll give you two personal experiences. In the first experience, I was taking a biology course at Compton College over the summer. There were several students in the class from surrounding universities who decided to take biology over the summer becuase we thought it would be easier. The instructor was an elderly White man and the majority of the students in the class were Black. On the first day of class, the instructor greeted each student while taking roll, and in the process, discussed our skeletal features. For me, he told me I looked Ethiopian but also had a bit of Mongolian in me. I was quite bothered by this, along with other students in the class. After class, we stood outside his door and discussed it. Fast forward, much of his instruction was highly disorganized and boring. We never did labs, never worked in small groups, it was 100% lecture. At the end of the class, many of us received a "D". We complained to the president of the school and our grades were adjusted. I could share more about this experience, but I just wanted you to see how these ideas manifest in today's world.

In the **second experience**, I visited the doctor with my mother. I chose to use a kid in the scenario, but this is based on an actual event. There are questions in the **Chapter Checkup** related to this story.

What Can Dr. Vinson Do to Help Mrs. Nell?

- **Think** - First, you will *think* about the problem. This entails identifying what is happening in the scenario and identifying the problem or issue. For our case studies, we want to be thinking about: *In which layer is racism potentially operating in this scenario?*

- **Respect** - Here, you will make the decision to *respect* those involved in the scenario. Any time we are working towards better understanding and getting ourselves and others to a better place, it's important that everyone's humanity is recognized and valued.

- **Empathy** - As we are working through each of the scenarios, we want to be aware of the opinions of others and their perspectives. Showing *empathy* means that you intentionally shift perspective and place yourself in someone else's situation.

- **Compassion** - Finally, we take a step in the direction of actually helping someone. When we show *compassion,* we are taking action. We will use this step to discuss the "what" and "how" you will help solve the problem.

Complete the TREC Method below. Remember, these case studies simply present dilemmas where an inequity might exist. Our goal is to work through each one and think about how we can support Dr. Vinson.

TREC Method

THINK:

RESPECT:

EMPATHY:

COMPASSION:

CHAPTER 2 CHECKUP

1. After reading the **Doctor Visit** story, what are you wondering about as it relates to the conversation between the patient and the doctor?

2. Conduct an Internet search on "University of Washington Medicine Exclude Race Calculation". Read the article and write a short reflection below.

3. What are some steps you think Dr. Vinson can take to address this issue? Feel free to use your notes from the TREC Method on the previous page. Remember, the goal is to demonstrate compassion.

4. The NFL recently agreed to end "race-based adjustments in testing retired players for dementia". Conduct an Internet search on the topic. Are there similarities with the **Doctor Visit** story?

5. What are some of the potential harms African American face when medical professionals use a factor specifically for African Americans?

FISHBONE GROUP ACTIVITY

INSTRUCTIONS:

(If in a group setting, complete as a group. If not, complete independently)

Step 1: Get in a group of 4 to 5

Step 2: Draw an image of a fish bone similar to the picture below

Step 3: Discuss your reflections from the chapter

Step 4: On the head of the fish, write **Ideological Racism**

Step 5: On the left side of the image, write potential issues related to **Ideological Racism**

Step 6: For each issue on the left, write solutions on the right for each issue on the left

Endnotes

1   George M. Fredrickson, *Racism: A Short History*(New Jersey: Princeton University Press, 2002), 5.

2   A.C. DE C.M. Saunders, *A Social History of Black Slaves and Freedmen in Portugal 1441-1555* (New York: Cambridge University Press), 36.

3   Fredrickson, *Racism: A Short History,* 36.

4   Tommie Shelby, "Ideology, Racism, and Critical Social Theory," *The Philosophical Forum* Vol XXXIV, no. 2(2003).

5   Saunders, *A Social History of Black Slaves and Freedmen,* 35.

6   Gomes Eanes De Zurara, *The Chronicle of the Discovery and Conquest of Guinea* (New York: Cambridge University Press, 2010).

7   Saunders, *A Social History of Black Slaves and Freedmen,* 5.

8   Gomes Eanes De Zurara, *The Chronicle of the Discovery and Conquest of Guinea* (New York: Cambridge University Press, 2010),

9   Jason Murdock, "Humans Have More Than 6,000 Thoughts per Day, Psychologists Discover," Newsweek. Newsweek, July 15, 2020. https://www.newsweek.com/humans-6000-thoughts-every-day-1517963.

10   DuBois T. McMillan, The World's Easiest Mini-Book on Improving your Memory Using Memory Palaces (Los Angeles: QuestVersity, 2021).

11   Ann Monroe Joel Amidon, "Education, Society, & the K-12 Learner," Lumen, accessed August 20, 2021, https://courses.lumenlearning.com/teachereducationx92x1/chapter/piagets-theory-of-cognitive-development

12   Sally Haslanger, *Resisting Reality* (New York: Oxford University Press, 2012), 174.

13   Saunders, *A Social History of Black Slaves and Freedmen,* 35.

14   Ibid, 5.

16   Ibid, 81.

17   Ibid, 84.

18   Ibid, 35 - 45.

19   Ibid, 37.

20   Myron P. Gutmann, "The Origins of the Thirty Years' War," accessed August 20, 2021, https://www.jstor.org/stable/204823.

21   John Rolfe, "'Twenty and Odd Negroes'; an Excerpt from a Letter from John Rolfe to Sir Edwin Sandys (1619/1620)," Encyclopedia Virginia, accessed August 20, 2021, https://encyclopediavirginia.org/entries/twenty-and-odd-negroes-an-excerpt-from-a-letter-from-john-rolfe-to-sir-edwin-sand-ys-1619-1620/.

22   "Wessell Webling, His Indenture (1622)." n.d. www.latinamericanstudies.org. Accessed September 21, 2021. https://www.latinamericanstudies.org/united-states/indentured-contract.htm.

23   Jacqueline Battalora, *Birth of a White Nation* (Houston, TX: Strategic Book Publishing, 2013), 17-27.

24   Ibid, 2.

25   Joy Degruy, *Post Traumatic Slavery Syndrome: America's Legacy of Enduring Injury and Healing* (Joy DeGruy, 2017).

26   Ibid, 57.

27   John Haller, *Outcasts from Evolution: Scientific Attitudes of Racial Inferiority, 1859-1900* (Illinois: Southern Illinois University Press, 1971), 4.

28   Fredrickson, *Racism: A Short History,* 6.

29   Ibid, 6.

30   Haller, *Outcasts from Evolution: Scientific Attitudes of Racial Inferiority, 1859-1900,* 4-5.

31   Ibid, 5.

32   Ibid, 6.

Chapter 3
Structural Racism

Institutions are situated in bigger structures.

The purpose of this chapter is to help you become familiar with the structural layer of racism, which is usually hidden, embedded in institutions, and operates systemically in a complex network of systems that perpetuate inequities.

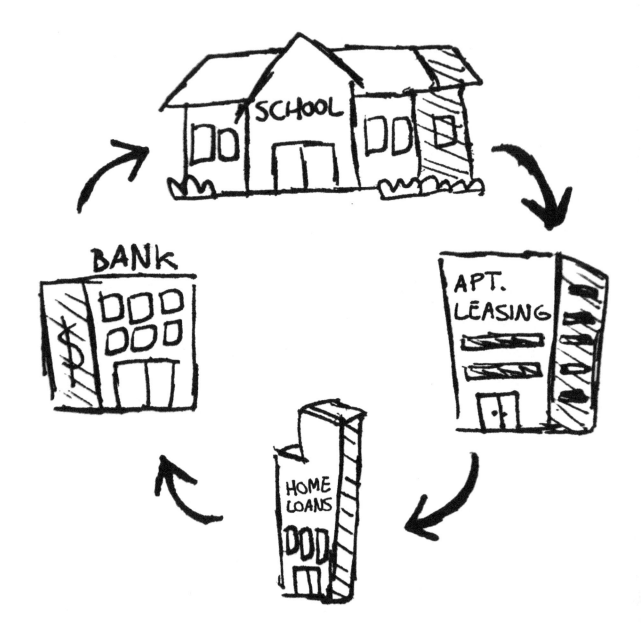

- understand structural racism in the U.S. and how it operates
- construct your own definition of structural racism
- analyze statistical outcomes and discuss the effects of structural racism on society
- understand how ideological racism informs structural racism
- identify how structural racism is operating in a life-like scenario and develop a plan to address it

...materials needed

- access to the Internet

Political systems
Laws   Court Cases
National values
            Public Policies
State rulings
            Constitution
Cultural representations

Structural Racism

Seeing or experiencing racism is one thing. But, to know it is happening and not know where it is coming from is another.

Introduction: Structural Racism

When I think of structural racism, I think of a network of institutions in which cultural norms, public policies, and institutional practices work together and function to perpetuate racial inequity to ensure the group with power, stays in power. Major institutions such as education, banking, law, real estate, politics, and many others are situated within a bigger social structure such as the one here in the United States, which sets the framework and rules by which these institutions function. These might include government agencies, economic systems, or even ideological frameworks.

In this chapter, we will be exploring structural racism in a short scenario, thinking about how it operates and plays out. You will then reflect, think, and apply your knowledge in a life-like simulation using the TREC Approach. The goal is for you to develop a clear understanding of structural racism which will set the groundwork for understanding what we mean when we say we are becoming anti-racist in our work, our homes, our communities, our nation, and our world.

"Structural racism is a network of institutions working to give advantages to the group in power."

■   ■   ■

Timothy Farmer is an African American man who was discharged from the U.S. Army in 1953 after his tour in the Korean War. Two years prior, President Truman signed Executive Order 9981 to desegregate the armed forces. As a kid, Timothy was fascinated about electronic radios, and though he only finished school up to the 8th grade, he was ecstatic when he met an older relative who told him about what he could learn in the military. He shared how they would teach him responsibility, hard work, and they might even teach him how to fly a plane. Full of excitement and a burning desire to leave his segregated town, Timothy took his advice and enlisted in the Army when he turned 18. He thought to himself, "There's not much happening here in this small town, why not go and explore something new?" Timothy completed basic training in eight weeks and became a member of an all Black battalion. He encountered racism as a soldier; some experiences were blatant such as when a waiter in a small restaurant refused to serve him and his Black friend, but allowed White soldiers to enter and eat at the counter. This angered Timothy. Though he knew following along could keep him alive, it just didn't feel right to be mistreated like that, after all, "I'm a man just like them."

When the war broke out in 1950, his battalion was sent to South Korea and some time later engaged in a fierce battle with the Chinese that ended in several of the men being killed. When the war was over, Timothy completed his term in the military and returned home.

During his transition back to Tupelo, MS, he became extremely frustrated at the racist climate lingering in the small town and he could still feel the suffocating presence of Jim Crow-ism in the air which made him anxious; segregation felt like a sticky mist that permeated the air. Though he had represented his country in a bloody war, he became disenchanted with sitting in the back of the bus, having to enter restaurants through the back door, and being treated like a second class citizen.

Timothy traveled to Cleveland, OH, and met up with a young beautiful woman from his hometown who had moved to Cleveland with a cousin. They soon married and moved to sunny southern California to explore opportunities. One of Timothy's older brothers was already in Los Angeles and encouraged him to move to the Oakwood area of Venice. He liked Venice because the homes were tidy and everyone seemed to take care of their lawns, and he knew he would eventually start a family, so being in a good school district was also important. The biggest attraction was that it was *near the beach. On a bright day, he went to three builders in the area and was shocked that all three told him there were no more homes in their inventories. Timothy felt in his gut that the men were lying, especially when Timothy caught a glimpse of a flyer inserted into an open notebook with "Restrictive Covenants" in bold lettering at the bottom. Timothy became frustrated, and what seemed like a promising new experience, began feeling like the some old racialized society he knew so well. Instead of pressing the issue and making a big fuss, he took the advice of a fellow veteran and drove to Compton, CA, the next weekend as a prospective place to live. Timothy was told that this area was open to Blacks and he wouldn't have to worry about restrictive covenants. Timothy didn't know much about how to finance the purchase a house, but his friend told him the VA would guide him through the entire process. After touring a house and chatting with a few of the neighbors who were also from the south and recently transplanted to Compton, he felt comfortable and excited that he would become a homeowner.*

Timothy and his wife purchased a three bedroom, one bath home in a quaint neighborhood in West Compton. Timothy decided to go with the finance company recommended by the builder. He didn't mind paying a few more dollars a month, he just wanted to own a home and the builder seemed nice and welcoming and told him exactly which bank to go to. After all, he had heard about Blacks getting turned away from developments that were backed by FHA and VA, and he didn't feel like fussing with people over "programs that ain't created for people like me no way."

Timothy started his new job in electronics and prepared to start a family. He knew he had to get additional training in electronics so he enrolled in a local private school for adults that accepted Blacks, though there was a local community college closer to Timothy's house. Timothy wasn't sure if they accepted Blacks, so he continued at the private school for Blacks and completed the program.

Timothy worked in the aerospace industry for 40 years and received many awards for his achievements.

As mentioned, this story was inspired by my father's journey through the segregated south, the military, and his eventual move to California where he experienced even more subtle forms of discrimination.

Before we reflect on Timothy's story, I want you to conduct a brief search on racially restrictive covenants. The University of Washington has an extensive digital catalog on this topic. Type the following into the address bar of your browser: **https://depts.washington.edu/civilr/covenants.htm** and scroll to the bottom of the page. If it's not available use a search engine and type in: restrictive covenants University of Washington. Read through some of the documents and answer the question below:

What wording do you consistently see in the documents pertaining to restrictive covenants?

Activity #1: Discuss in Groups (or as an individual reflection)

1. What biases do you think Timothy is confronted with in this case study?

2. Describe how you think Timothy felt when he returned home from the Korean War.

3. What stopped Timothy from moving to Venice?

4. Do you have any additional wonderings about Timothy and his outlook?

Structural Racism

As we explore structural racism, it's important to note that structural racism is informed by ideological racism (covered in the previous chapter), which is a set of beliefs that uses physical, ethnic, or cultural differences to justify one group's goal to oppress another. This creates a maldistribution of resources, restricts certain groups from having adequate access to opportunities, and continues to normalize inequity and promote the outcomes they produce as evidence that the group racialized as White is simply better by nature. Structural racism is embedded into how society is built and is often hidden. We typically see racism rear its ugly head through our experiences with policies, procedures, and practices at the institutional, cultural, or interpersonal levels. If we are to become **antiracist**, we must be able to understand how structural racism functions in order to call it out, address it, and disrupt it.

"Structural racism is embedded into how society is built and often hidden. We typically see racism rear its ugly head through our experiences with policies, procedures, and practices at the institutional, cultural, or interpersonal levels."

Before we take a dive into structural racism in the United States, I want to clarify a few things before we get started. We may have all heard of the terms: structural racism, systematic racism, and systemic racism, and these labels are often used to describe the same thing and I want to draw some distinction between them before we go forward. My view is not the only view and I'm not professing that my definition is the "correct" way of viewing these words, the definitions I offer will simply help us understand what I'm presenting in this chapter.

Structural - Systemic - Systematic Racism

First, when I think of structural racism I think of the "design" of systems. Not so much the physical structure, but the rules and policies put in place. They are the structures that we interface with and function in, they are essentially the rules of the game. Structures answer the "what" question. You might ask, "What type of structures? They might be a political system, legal system, educational system, economic system, health system, and many others. Where I see structure dealing more with the design, I see "systemic" as examining how something operates between and within these systems. For instance, when the human body has a virus, the virus isn't isolated to one part of the body, it affects the entire body and flows through the bloodstream, just as racism does in the United States. The word *system* comes from the Greek word sistēma which is a composition, or a set of individual parts working together or making up a whole. Lastly, systematic racism, which is often used interchangeably for structural or systemic racism, would mean that there's a method or process to racism. If we think of the layers of racism forming in a chronological fashion or through some methodology or steps, then that might be called "systematic racism". My focus in this chapter is on how the design (structure) of racism affects people and how it works and operates (systemically) between and through systems of oppression. Again, you might hear these words used interchangeably, and that also works, but I'll attempt to delineate between them for purposes of clarity and accuracy.

Structural racism in the United States is a network of inequity that gives people racialized as White unfair access and opportunities over people racialized in a non-White category, because Whites are the only group able to harness the accumulated power attained in all five layers of racism (ideological, structural, institutional, cultural, individual). This layer is informed by the ideological layer and operates to reinforce and perpetuate white supremacy through norms and practices. Racism works in one direction, so those people racialized as White are the only group that has the collective and accumulative power to oppress other groups by definition. We will examine this idea a bit later, but for now, take a look at the diagram below that illustrates how structural racism worked to keep Timothy from accessing the same opportunities as Whites.

As mentioned, structural racism is a network of institutions working together to give advantages to the group in power. Here, we see a collective system of inequity operating systemically and restricting him from opportunities that have been set aside for a specific group. State laws prevented him from entering the front door of a restaurant, the Federal Housing Authority's (FHA) guidelines on lending encouraged unfair practices in the real estate industry such as restrictive covenants, and segregation in public schools discouraged him from attending a local community college. We will look at these individual institutions in the next chapter, but for now, remember that the ideological layer (covered in the previous chapter), continuously informs and feeds other layers of oppression, or inner layers, of racism. It's also important to point out the accumulation of power that is being exercised here. Everywhere Timothy turns, he faces racism. That's what makes it systemic, it's everywhere! Let's revisit the image from the beginning of the chapter.

Activity #2: Personal Reflection (Venn Chart)

In the **Venn Chart** below, write details on how **Ideological Racism** and **Structural Racism** are different in the outer circles and how they are similar where the circles overlap.

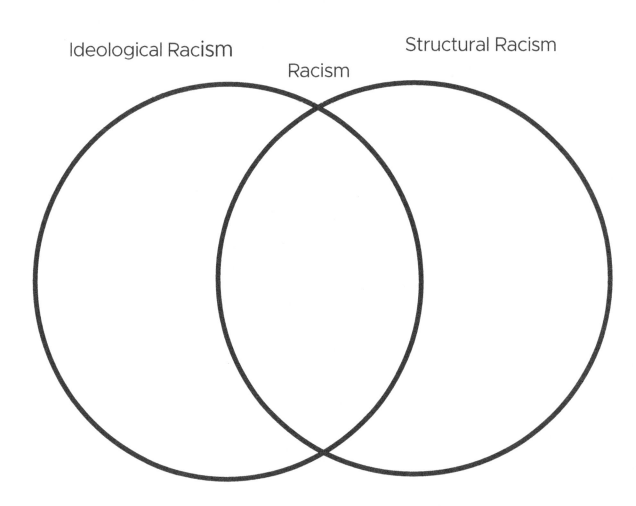

Ideological Racism

Racism

Structural Racism

Ideology Informing Structures

Racism is entrenched and deeply rooted in the social structures in the United States. There is a vast body of work on the study of structural racism and how it produces outcomes that are consistent with the belief of white racial superiority. At the center of this complex notion, is the contradictory idea that all people are "created equal" and should have the freedom to live as they please. As we know, from early colonial times through the mid-19th century, this only applied to men classified as "white". Just as we saw racist ideology form to justify the enslavement of West Africans by the Portuguese as early as the 1400s, through legitimization from religious authorities (popes) and kings, by turning expeditions into crusades and granting plenary indulgence to remove sin and any guilt, we see this power used to serve Whites economically, socially, and politically in the pursuit of what the early colonists called *freedom*. Let's take a look at some of the papal bulls passed in the 15th century (1400s) and then explore some of the laws passed during early colonial times in Virginia and Maryland. These two colonies had much influence on the ideology and forming of the United States as evident in four of the first five Presidents coming from Virginia. We will see how these legal actions, in the form of edicts and laws, shaped the ideological frameworks that influenced attitudes and social behaviors.

Historian Jacqueline Battalora nailed the point on how laws influence behavior when she wrote, "laws help us understand the broad social context in which we exist" and is a "legitimizing institution."[1] Laws are critical in how we interact in our social world. They protect us, keep us from harm and danger, give us rights and liberties, and help to govern behaviors in our society. There are a host of other benefits that laws give us, I just listed a few here.

In the previous chapter, we explored some of the moves made by Prince Henry the Navigator to legitimize his efforts, and he found this support from the church and the king. More specifically, this occurred after successful expeditions south of Cape Bojador where he returned with gold and natives in 1441 and 1442. He appealed "directly to the whole body of Christian sovereigns for aid in discovery and conquest."[2] These official orders gave the conquests "purpose" that extended beyond personal greed to one that sought to fulfill God's will. Zurara stated this clearly when he identified the five reasons for Prince Henry's conquest of Guinea:

- "his zeal for the service of God";
- to find some Christians to trade with;
- to determine how far the power of the Moors (infidels) extended;
- to find a Christian king in this land after warring with the Moors for "one hundred and thirty years;
- "to make increase in the faith of our Lord Jesus Christ and to bring to him all the souls that should be saved."[3]

Papal bulls Illius Qui, Dum Diversas, and bull Romanus Pontifex were issued in the mid-1400s and gave him the backing needed to conquer non-Christian lands. A papal bull is a decree or edict signed by the pope of the Catholic Church in the form of a letter that contained a seal that made it official. Here are key excerpts from each of the documents:

- bull Illius qui (1442): Granted full remission of sins and declared the Portuguese expeditions down the coast of Africa to be a crusade.

- bull Dum Diversas (1452): "Authorizes the king to make war upon the infidels, to conquer their lands, and to enslave their persons."[4]

- bull Romanus Pontifex (1455): "Granted King Alfonso general and indefinite powers to search out and conquer all pagans, enslave them and appropriate their lands and goods."[5]

These edicts were passed down by the Catholic Church in the 15th Century and gave rise to the conquering of lands and people outside of Europe, subjecting people to perpetual servitude, and building economic wealth for the sole purpose of global domination under the guise of "Christianizing" the world. As a result, some studies that suggest, upwards of 12 millions Africans were kidnapped and brought to America, many died in the initial contact with Europeans or en route.[6] Additionally, genocide was inflicted on Indigenous people of the land now called America.

Let's take a look at how these events in history impacted lives. I know it's impossible to read the document, I simply inserted it for viewing purposes so that you will know that this document actually exists. You will conduct an Internet search in the next activity and learn about each papal bull. See figure 1 below.

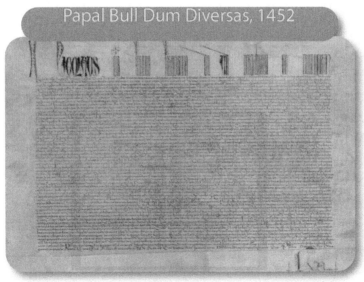

Figure 1. Image of papal bull Dum Diversas. Retrieved from Indigenous Values, "Dum Diversas," Doctrine of Discovery, July 23, 2018, https://doctrineofdiscovery.org/dum-diversas/

Activity #3: Analyze and Annotate (Individual)

Conduct an Internet search of the three papal bulls listed above. Jot down key words that you feel support the notion that Africans and non-Christians were being targeted, singled-out, or exploited. Write three questions or wonderings that you would pose to the author of this edict.

Conduct an Internet Search
(Write down notes for each)

bull Illius Qui:

bull Dum diversas:

bull Romanus pontifex:

- Question One:

- Question Two:

- Question Three:

Activity #4: Reflection (Group or Individual)

Answer the following questions below in small groups of three to four. The purpose of these questions is to spark conversation on what we covered. There are no right or wrong answers, but it would be great if the dialogue is centered on what we covered in this section.

1. What does it mean to have plenary indulgence?

2. How do you think Henry the Navigator felt after getting support from the Catholic Church?

3. Is there a connection between the contents of these documents and racist ideology (see Chapter 2)? If so, in what ways?

4. In what ways do you think these documents influenced the Trans-Atlantic Slave Trade?

5. **Read the story on the next page and answer the questions that follow.**

Katherine is a White woman who recently completed her doctorate in Special Education from a top-tier university in northern California. She is looking to take the leap into administration for a small to middle-size school district. After living in the Bay area all of her life, she thought a change of scenery was long overdue, and besides, the thought of hot sandy beaches in bright, sunny Southern California had just the right mix of great weather and night life that gave her instant euphoria. Now in her early 30s, Katherine was still in touch with some of her closest friends from her undergraduate days. Pamela, a roommate from college, lived in Los Angeles and invited her to come out and visit her, "It'll be cool. Just come on out and we'll have a blast. I'll take you around, show you the city and get you in contact with friends of mine who are in education," Pamela said, bubbling in excitement over the phone. Katherine scheduled her flight and arrived in Los Angeles a few weeks later.

After two full days of driving around the city, shopping, looking at prospective living options, Katherine was sold on the idea of moving to Los Angeles. Pamela connected her with a friend who was a principal at a local district and was able to get Katherine an interview. Katherine was thankful. She applied for the position online and began preparing for the interview, which was to be conducted the very next day because the end-date for interviews was nearing. Katherine was excited, everything was going quite well and she thanked Pamela for her hospitality and for making the connection with the principal. The next day, Katherine arrived early for the interview. She watched the students entering the main gate of the school. She couldn't help but notice that all of the students were Hispanic or African American. This didn't bother Katherine at all, she was prepared to teach all kids. That was one of the reasons she decided to become an educator in the first place.

Katherine entered the campus and was greeted by the staff. She immediately felt their warmth and thought how great it would be to become part of the team. Katherine was interviewed by a panel of four, which included the principal, a teacher, the counselor, and a parent. During the interview, Katherine did quite well.

She answered all of the questions concisely, made references to researched-based practices, and interjected her personal experiences at certain times to demonstrate her depth of knowledge, skills, and understanding of the role of a 21st Century school leader.

Katherine did notice one thing in the interview that made her a bit uneasy, and it didn't dawn on her until she received a phone call the next day and the person said, "We would like to thank you for considering a position with our school, but we have chosen someone else for the position. We wish you the best of luck and please check our website for openings in the future." Of the questions posed to Katherine in the interview, she felt there was a strong emphasis on the cultural backgrounds of the students, and perhaps she wasn't chosen because she was White. Katherine was upset and said to Pamela, "That's racist. I think they didn't hire me because I'm White."

Activity #5: Reflection (Group or Individual)

There are some interesting dynamics occurring in this case study. Before answering the question below, think about the Timothy Farmer case study and see if similar things are operating in Katherine's story.

1. Based on information provided in the case study and what we have learned about racism, is racism operating here? State evidence.

2. In what ways can Katherine support her claim that racism was used in this case?

3. Based on what you know about structural (systemic) racism, please explain how this case is different from Tommy Farmer's case.

Again, what we are examining is *a total system of inequity* called racism. We break it down into layers so that we can analyze how it operates in various forms so that we can deconstruct it at these levels and stop it from operating. This approach is like having the 'check engine' light go on in your car. You might not know where the problem stems from, but some sensor in the car's system tells you there is a problem. The mechanic connects it to a diagnostic device and the device gives him/her a reading that tells them exactly what is wrong with your car. That's how we want to examine racism. We want to run it through our critical anti-racist lens so that we can identify it, create a plan to get rid of it, and execute the plan.

In order to apply some critical thinking to Katherine's case, it is important to contextualize what it means to be "white" in America. We will see how whiteness is constructed through a legal process. They operate within the outer layer (ideology) and represent the rules that govern us. They provide the infrastructure and big vision for our country. Let's get back to Bacon's Rebellion.

Back to the Bacon Rebellion

During early colonial times, many Blacks were brought to the newly occupied land as indentured servants. Alongside many whites who were sent from Europe to the colonies, they worked on tobacco farms as laborers, many under contracts that guaranteed land upon completion of the contract. For example, in the indentured contract between Wessell Webling and Edward Bennett, we see that Webling was to receive "a house and 50 acres of land". Nathaniel Bacon, a successful farmer, demanded support from the governor of Virginia, William Berkeley, who happened to be a relative of Bacon. Bacon felt Berkeley wasn't responsive to his plea to take action against Native Americans for raiding the colony and wanted to retaliate. By not taking swift action, Bacon believed this threatened his ability to expand and acquire new land. As Michelle Alexander puts it, Native Americans "became a growing impediment to white European progress".[7] So, Bacon "organized his own militia, consisting of White and Black indentured servants and enslaved black people" and they attacked nearby Native Americans in exchange for the promise of freedom.[8] After their attacks on Natives, they went to the capital of Virginia in Jamestown and burned it down.

The notion of having Blacks and Whites coming together and revolting against White landowners was a threat to the colony. According to Jacqueline Battalora, Blacks and whites faced similar conditions while working as laborers in the colonies.[9] This changed quickly after the rebellion. Virginia lawmakers passed laws to separate the two groups. They did this by identifying Europeans as "white" and shifting their focus to only place Africans into perpetual servitude.

As figure 2 shows, many of these laws targeted Africans and Native Americans, restricting them of basic rights. Additionally, table 1 shows how these legal actions affected the population of Africans in the colony from 1625 to 1775.

Laws Enacted in Virginia During the Early Colonial Period that Targeted Africans and Native Americans

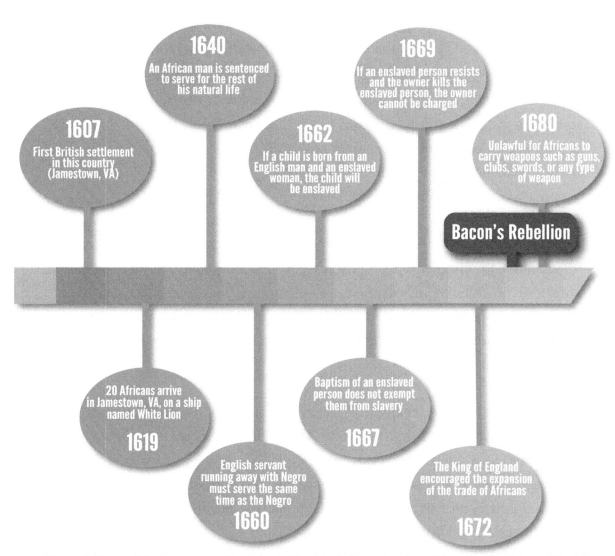

1640
An African man is sentenced to serve for the rest of his natural life

1669
If an enslaved person resists and the owner kills the enslaved person, the owner cannot be charged

1607
First British settlement in this country (Jamestown, VA)

1662
If a child is born from an English man and an enslaved woman, the child will be enslaved

1680
Unlawful for Africans to carry weapons such as guns, clubs, swords, or any type of weapon

Bacon's Rebellion

20 Africans arrive in Jamestown, VA, on a ship named White Lion
1619

Baptism of an enslaved person does not exempt them from slavery
1667

English servant running away with Negro must serve the same time as the Negro
1660

The King of England encouraged the expansion of the trade of Africans
1672

Figure 2. Many of the laws enacted in Colonial Virginia. Information from "Slave Law in Colonial Virginia: A Timeline." Retrieved from https://www.shsu.edu/~jll004/vabeachcourse_spring09/bacons_rebellion/

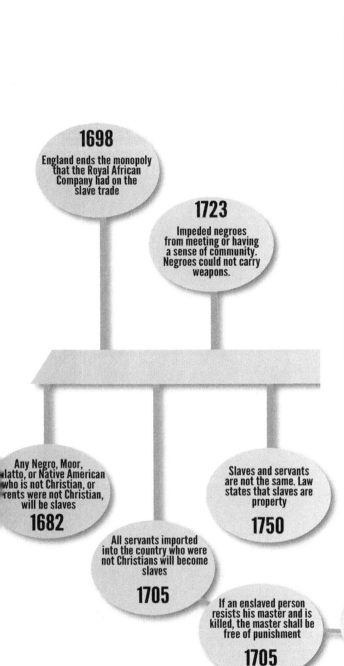

Black Population in Virginia from 1625 to 1775	
1625	23
1648	300
1671	2,000
1680	3,000
1700	16,390
1720	26,559
1730	30,000
1740	60,000
1775	210,000

Table 1. Population of Africans in the Virginia colony from 1625 to 1775. Data from "Slave Law in Colonial Virginia: A Timeline."

1698
England ends the monopoly that the Royal African Company had on the slave trade

1723
Impeded negroes from meeting or having a sense of community. Negroes could not carry weapons.

Any Negro, Moor, mulatto, or Native American who is not Christian, or parents were not Christian, will be slaves
1682

All servants imported into the country who were not Christians will become slaves
1705

If an enslaved person resists his master and is killed, the master shall be free of punishment
1705

No minister shall marry a white man with a negro or mulatto woman, or a white woman with a negro or mulatto man
1705

Slaves and servants are not the same. Law states that slaves are property
1750

Activity #6: Analyzing Data (Group or Individual)

The timeline and population data on the previous pages give us some insight on what was happening in the Virginia colony in the 17th and 18th centuries. You will analyze the timeline and data and answer the questions below.

1. What trends do you see happening in the data?

2. Is there any particular law passed during this period that is more surprising than others to you? Why?

3. Explain the huge jump in the population of Blacks from 1680 to 1700.

4. In what specific ways do you think these laws influenced the population of Blacks in Virginia during this time?

The purpose of these laws was clear: to place Whites, Africans, and Native in specific legal categories; elevate the status of Whites; and ensure Africans and Natives were completely dominated by Whites and never bonded together with indentured servants to fight against the interest of the colonists. This strategy proved to be effective for the colonists. While elevating the status of all Whites, these Virginia laws regulated Blacks to perpetual slavery without the possibility of freedom, made it illegal for them to carry firearms, marry Whites, testify against Whites in court, and a host of other limitations.

Helping Katherine with her Concerns

Before revisiting the case study, use the **TREC Method** to help guide your response to Katherine. You will be playing the role of her friend, Pamela.

Using the TREC Method to address the dilemma

What should Pamela be thinking about?

THINK:

How can Pamela ensure she shows respect as she tries to address the problem?

RESPECT:

How can Pamela demonstrate empathy for Katherine in this dilemma?

EMPATHY:

What are some ways in which Pamela might show compassion by helping Katherine?

COMPASSION:

CHAPTER 3 CHECKUP

1. Racist ideology informs structures. These structures set the rules that we live by and affect every aspect of our lives

True ☐   False ☐

2. Which of the following are ways structural racism operates in our country?

☐ federal laws

☐ state laws

☐ court rulings

☐ national values

3. The reaction to the Bacon Rebellion resulted in the enactment of laws that restricted the rights and movement of Africans.

True ☐   False ☐

4. What is the difference between ideological racism and structural racism?

5. Does anyone on the Katherine's interview panel have the accumulated power to be racist towards Katherine by not offering her the job because she is White? Explain you answer.

DEAR PENNSYLVANIA LEGISLATURE ACTIVITY

Read the excerpt from one of the first antiracist protests in the the U.S.

> GERMANTOWN FRIENDS' PROTEST AGAINST SLAVERY, 1688.
>
> *"These are the reasons why we are against the traffick of men-body, as followeth. Is there any that would be done or handled at this manner?"...*
>
> *"There is a saying, that we shall doe to all men like as we will be done ourselves; making no difference of what generation, descent or colour they are. And those who steal or robb men, and those who buy or purchase them, are they not all alike?"...*
>
> *"But to bring men hither, or to rob and sell them against their will, we stand against."[10]*

Slavery was obviously unsettling for many people for obvious reasons. The excerpt above proves that there were people who protested the mistreatment of Africans. Based on what you know now about structural racism, construct a simple letter on the next page to the Pennsylvania Legislature in the mid-1600s that highlights the dangers of structural racism and how it is used to normalize the dehumanization of people.

Write a short letter in the space below:

Endnotes

1   Jacqueline Battalora, *Birth of a White Nation,* 3.

2   Raymond C. Beazley, "Prince Henry of Portugal and the African Crusade of the Fifteenth Century." *The American Historical Review* 16, no. 1 (1910): 11-23. Accessed August 21, 2021. doi:10.2307/1834305.

3   Gomes Eanes De Zurara, *The Chronicle of the Discovery and Conquest of Guinea* (New York: Cambridge University Press, 2010), 28-29.

4   Raymond C. Beazley, 16.

5   Frances G. Davenport, *European Treaties Bearing on the History of the United States and its Dependencies Vol. 1* (Washington, D.C.: Carnegie Institution of Washington, 1917), 12.

6   "Middle Passage." Slavery and Remembrance. Accessed August 21, 2021. http://slaveryandremembrance.org/articles/article/?id=A0032.

7   Michelle Alexander, *The New Jim Crow* (New York: New Press), 23.

8   "Inventing Black and White." 2013. Facing History and Ourselves. 2013. https://www.facinghistory.org/holocaust-and-human-behavior/chapter-2/inventing-black-and-white.

9   Jacqueline Battalora, *Birth of a White Nation.*

10   "Germantown Friends' Protest against SLAVERY 1688. [Facsimile].," The Library of Congress, accessed September 30, 2021, https://www.loc.gov/resource/rbpe.14000200/?st=text.

Chapter 4
Institutional Racism

Racism oftentimes operates in institutional policies and practices.

The purpose of this chapter is to introduce you to institutional racism and examine how racism operates within institutions and affects life experiences.

MODERN LANGUAGE OFFERINGS

- ☐ Spanish
- ☐ Latin
- ☐ Japanese
- ☐ French
- ☐ Italian

...what you will be able to do at the end of this chapter:

- understand institutional racism in the U.S. and how it operates
- construct your own definition of institutional racism
- analyze statistical outcomes and discuss the effects of institutional racism
- understand how ideological and structural racism inform institutional racism
- design a plan to address institutional racism in a life-like scenario

...materials needed for this chapter:

- access to the Internet

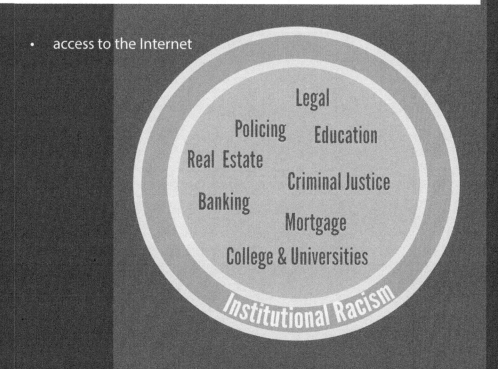

Legal

Policing   Education

Real Estate

Criminal Justice

Banking

Mortgage

College & Universities

Institutional Racism

The rules of the game are established by big frameworks (structures), but it's at the institutional level where these rules are enforced.

Introduction: Institutional Racism

As we saw in the previous chapter, racism is built into the various structures in the United States, and in turn, these strcutures inform institutions. The impact is widespread as we continue to see outcomes for non-Whites *continue to inform us of* the systemic nature of racism and how it operates inside, between, and through the various institutions that are situated in the bigger structures of our country such as our economic, legal, and political systems. When we face racism, we often see it at the institutional, cultural, or interpersonal layers. When we see it in institutions, it's usually in policies, procedures, or practices that advantage those who are members of the group in power.

Ibram Kendi believes a racist policy is "any policy that yields a racial inequity."

In this chapter, we will explore institutional racism. It is important to know that institutional racism is constantly informed by ideology and the structures in which it is situated.

We will be analyzing data, reviewing historical facts and have time to ponder and make sense of these facts, and look at a scenario where you will have an opportunity to reflect, think, and apply your knowledge in using the TREC approach.

■ ■ ■

Keila is in her senior year of high school and is excited after sitting down with her high school guidance counselor and looking through the course offerings to fulfill her requirements for graduation. She wants to earn her Seal of Biliteracy, but not sure if it's going to give her that extra boost to get into some of the top colleges. At this point, she's certain that she wants to attend a college out of state and has already been accepted through early admittance. Mrs. Hanson recommends that she takes the fourth year of Latin because "it'll look better on [her] application." Keila really wants to take the new African American Literature course, and really respects Mrs. Hanson's advice, so she goes to her office during lunch to discuss this with Mrs. Hanson.

```
FADE IN:

INT. HIGH SCHOOL COUNSELING OFFICE - DAY

KEILA, African-American female, 17, with long braids,
enters her counselor's, MRS. HANSON, office. Keila is
carrying a folder in hand and looks ANXIOUS.

CUT TO: CLOSE UP of Mrs. Hanson, 50ish, and wearing THICK
BIFOCAL GLASSES. She is flipping through files on her desk.
Her head is TILTED DOWN, she's focused intently on the
files.

                    MRS. HANSON
               (mumbling to herself)
          Let's see, I have Malik, Jazmine, Jacob…oh
          my god - let me start over again, this is
          so confusing…okay…

CUT TO: MEDIUM SHOT OF KEILA TAKING A SEAT IN FRONT OF MRS.
HANSON, but Mrs. Hanson, with her head still tilted down
and engrossed in the files, doesn't see or recognize Keila.

A MENACING FROWN spreads across Keila's face. Keila gives
off a long SIGH and FOLDS HER ARMS.

                    KEILA
               (to herself)
          This don't make no sense.

               (raises her voice)

          Mrs. Hanson…

CLOSE-UP of Hanson. Her EYES ARE BULGING, she's surprised.

                    MRS. HANSON

          Keila, you scared the daylights out of me,
          you can't - did you knock on the door?

                    KEILA

          I mean, I knocked like four times and you
          didn't answer so I just came in like I
          always do.

                    MRS. HANSON

          Oh, I'm sorry Keila. This college trip has
          me so stressed out. I mean, there's like
```

Keila's Dilemma

fifty kids going…hotels, buses, flights,
so much to do…

Keila has a PUZZLED LOOK on her face

                    MRS. HANSON

So, what's up? Need to talk about the
trip. I have your stuff…

MRS. Hanson FINGERS through the files.

                    MRS. HANSON (Cont.)

I have yours right here. You're all set to go.

                    KEILA

That's not what I'm here for.

                    MRS. HANSON

Whew!!! Good, I haven't been able to get
through your file yet anyway.

                    KEILA
                (mumbling)
It figures…

                    MRS. HANSON

    Huh?

                    KEILA

    Nothing.

CUT TO: CLOSE UP on MRS. HANSON'S EYES, then on KEILA'S
EYES. There's SILENCE.

                    MRS. HANSON

    You okay?

                    KEILA
                (eyes wander)
    Uh, yeah.

MRS. HANSON EXHALES, finally puts files to the side

MRS. HANSON

Now, c'mon. I've known you for three
years. I know when there's something
bothering you. Look, you're doing quite well,
you're set. You're meeting all of the
requirements, GPA is 3.83, S-A-T is good.
When you pass all of these senior classes
you won't have anything to worry about. We
have you in AP LIT, Calculus, Latin…

KEILA

Well, that's it. Last time we talked I told
I wanted to take the African American
Literature class instead of Latin, and you
were all against it telling me how it didn't
count…

MRS. HANSON
(perplexed)
I did?

KEILA
Uh yeah, you did.

MRS. Hanson takes a LONG SIGH.

MRS. HANSON

I know dear. I know it's a tough decision.
But, to be honest, this class won't help you
much. It won't give you the boost you need
to get into a top college. The fourth year
of Latin would be much better.

Keila FROWNS.

KEILA

I guess you're right. I guess I'll just
take the Latin class.

Keila stands and motions to walk out.

KEILA
Bye Mrs. Hanson.

MRS. HANSON
See you later, Keila. Let's talk more about
it another day.

Activity #1: Discuss in Groups (or as an individual reflection)

1. What is the main dilemma in this case? What do you see?

2. What inequities do you think might be operating in this case?

3. What opportunities are there to get rid of any inequities presented in this case?

4. If you were in Mrs. Hanson's position, what would you do?

Institutional Racism

When racist ideology is operationalized (or in action) we see it manifest in institutions in the form of policies, procedures, and practices that might discriminate against others based on race. It's important to understand how ideology continuously informs institutions through a perpetual loop that is always active, but often hidden. Ibram Kendi believes a racist policy is "any policy that yields a racial inequity."[1] When we think about policy, it's rare that we see policies written that are explicit about how institutions intend to discriminate against groups. In other words, it's not likely that a restaurant or a store will post a sign that reads, "No Asians, Negroes or Mexicans Allowed". When policy is written and there's a certain outcome expected, it is often written in a way that's extremely difficult to claim intent to discriminate or harm another person. In these cases, we might say racism is an "institutionalized" form of racism, but as we now know, it goes deeper than that. Yes, we might see it operating within an institution, but it's important to know how it is situated in ideological and structural frames that operate like an invisible hand behind a curtain. When we see racism it typically rears its head in outcomes.

> "Institutional racism is hidden in many cases and informed by ideology and structural forms of racism."

So, to take advantage of a particular group of people (this is only an example), all one has to do is research their patterns, have the power to write policy, then write the policy to get the outcome you are looking for. For instance, let's say I wanted to create a rule around college entrance and I wanted to attract students from a particular cross-section of our society. I could conduct research on something like SAT scores and write entrance qualifications that favor particular groups and eliminate others. This is only an example, but you see how it doesn't openly exclude groups, but the results will tell us a very different story. That would be considered a racist policy. In many cases, no one is sitting behind a desk trying to come up with ways to exclude groups, but the outcomes of policies, practices, and institutional decisions might have a disparaging impact on particular groups.

Many institutions in the United States have failed to address disparate outcomes despite efforts from the government to eliminate unfairness in areas such as achievement in education, wealth accumulation, employment, and the criminal justice system. Institutional racism is hidden in many cases and informed by ideology and structural forms of racism, which allows racism to persist and outcomes for non-Whites to fall far behind Whites in many areas of life. Let's take a look at some of these outcomes.

Economic Disparities

Though there have been changes in our legal system that expands rights to all Americans, there hasn't been much change in how these groups (particularly Blacks) have fared when competing for wealth and resources in America. This can be contributed to the maldistribution of resources due to racism. Claude Anderson believes that "true racism exists only when one groups holds a disproportionate share of wealth and power over another group then uses those resources to marginalize, exploit, exclude, and subordinate the weaker group".[2] According to Dr. Anderson, Blacks owned one-half of 1% of the country's wealth in 1860, and you would think the numbers would increase over the years, but the numbers were relatively the same in 1990, 140 years later.[3] This is consistent with more recent research conducted by Mehrsa Baradaran in a 2018 article published by "Boston Review" where she stated, "more than 150 years later...blacks still own less than 2 percent of the wealth in the

United States."[4] Along the same line, Patrick Sharkey revealed in his book *Stuck in Place,* that 39% of African Americans were in the lowest 1/5th of overall income distribution in the 1970s in the U.S., and in 2000, the number in the lowest 1/5th was 33%.[5] Things were no better for African Americans in the highest income distribution level; 8% of African Americans were at this level in 1970, and in 2010 the number had only increased to 9%. Sharkey also asserted that African American men have shown no growth based on the study. One of the most startling pieces of data came from a 2007 study conducted by Julia Isaacs. The study revealed that 45 percent of Black children whose parents were in the middle income distribution group ($48,800 - $81,200 per year) ended up at the bottom of the income distribution, whereas only 17 percent of White children dropped to the same level.[6] Adding to this, according to a report published by the Federal Reserve Bureau in 2016, the median net worth of a White family was $171,000, $20,700 for a Hispanic family, and only $17,600 for an African American family.[7] These numbers are important because they reveal how an inequity, likely caused by racism in this case, might still be operating and rendering results that clearly show Whites getting much more favorable outcomes over other groups.

Activity #2: Reflect on Data

White Family
net worth: 171k
in 2016

African American Family
net worth: 17.6k
in 2016

1. Which piece of data sticks out to you? Why?

2. What do you think are the specific causes for these disparities?

Conduct an Internet search and find another disparity in outcomes between Whites and another group. Use a credible source.

Convict Lease System

The origin of what we think of as modern day policing in the U.S. was established in the early 1700s. It was specifically established to capture runaway Africans who were enslaved to return them to their owners, where force and violence were typically used.[8] This system remained in place until slavery ended and turned into a similar system under what was called Black Codes, which expanded into segregation laws that became known as Jim Crow.

One of the keys to the success of Jim Crow-ism was the use of racism in state laws that worked in the favor of southern white landowners. The phrase Jim Crow comes from a minstrel song performed by a White actor by the name of Thomas Rice in the 1820s. It's important to know that slavery was still legal in the United States in the 1820s. Minstrel shows were characterized by White actors painting their faces black and ridiculing Black people.

At the end of the Civil War, many newly freed men and women remained in close proximity to their previous owners. One dynamic that remained, and held the vestiges of the past, was the relationships of those with power and those without power. Blackmon touched on this when he stated, "[slaves] were taught that their master was a palpable extension of the power of God – their designated lord in a supremely ordained hierarchy".[9] The 13th Amendment to the Constitution abolished slavery, "except as punishments for crime whereof the party shall have been duly convicted, shall exist in the United States, nor any place subject to their jurisdiction."[10] This loophole created another form of servitude where states profited from thousands of Blacks who were targeted and thrown in jail for the most ridiculous reasons such as vagrancy (homelessness) or for not having a job. This system become so lucrative, according to Robert Perkinson, author of *Tough Texas,* the state of Alabama received 73% of its revenue from prison contracts in 1898.[11] In many cases, the courts were used to settle civil debts and labor substituted for currency to pay fines and other fees owed to the court. Needless to say, this system was extremely profitable for the states involved.

The demand for cheap labor skyrocketed, and with this new state penal system of exploitation, landowners and companies rushed to the southern states to capitalize on this opportunity. Having a highly skilled workforce, coupled with legal practices that classified many crimes as misdemeanors, the new model for forced labor "significantly funded the operations of government by converting black forced labor into funds for the counties and states". These laws were specifically written for Black people and the convict lease system as "one of the harshest and most exploitative labor systems known in American history."[12] Most of the workers worked in coal mines, railroads, and large plantations. The conditions were so harsh that one in every four Blacks subjected to this system died.

Cycle of Servitude after Slavery Ended

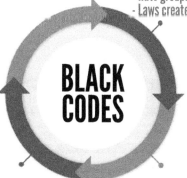

BLACK CODES

1865: Slavery was Abolished in the U.S.
- Formerly enslaved people had nowhere to go
- Hate groups formed to instill fear
- Laws created to keep them strapped to the land

Formerly Enslaved People Leased Back to Plantations
- Under similar conditions as they were during slavery
- Not protected by the law
- Generated revenue to southern states that were involved

Under the 13th Amendment
- Abolished slavery, unless convicted of a crime
- Could face criminal prosecution for crimes such as:
    - vagrancy
    - loitering
    - having weapons
    - unemployment
    - breaking curfew

Additionally, we are still seeing the proliferation of mass incarceration of Black and Hispanic men. Blacks and Hispanics makeup roughly 32% of the

BLACKS ARE 5 TIMES MORE LIKELY TO BE ARRESTED THAN WHITES

U.S. population, but account for 56% of those incarcerated in the U.S., and Blacks are 5 times more likely to be incarcerated than Whites. As we see, the 13th Amendment didn't provide much protection for Blacks. Racism is deeply entrenched in the system, and history has shown how it has adapted over time to maintain power imbalances that result in inequities in various institutions.

Activity #4: Analyzing Racism

1. In two words, how does learning about the convict lease system make you feel?

2. What form(s) of racism do you think are operating in the convict lease system?

	Layer	Evidence
☐	Ideological	
☐	Structural	
☐	Institutional	
☐	Cultural	
☐	Interpersonal	

3. How do you think officials in states that participated in this form of racism justified this system of exploitation?

4. What long-term impact do you think this had on Black families?

Books/Articles/Videos to Check Out		
Title	Author/Website	Type
Black Labor, White Wealth	Claud Anderson	Book
PowerNomics	Claud Anderson	Book
Stuck in Place	Patrick Sharkey	Book
Slavery by Another Name	Douglas Blackmon	Book
The New Jim Crow	Michelle Alexander	Book
What is Convict Leasing?	https://exhibits.library.rice.edu/exhibits/show/sugarlandconvictleasing/history-of-convict-leasing	Article
Southern Black Codes	https://www.crf-usa.org/brown-v-board-50th-anniversary/southern-black-codes.html	Article
Reconstruction: The Black Codes	https://ca.pbslearningmedia.org/resource/reconstruction-black-codes/reconstruction-the-black-codes/	Video

Racism in Housing

We've all heard this phrase in regards to wealth: *"If you want to get rich or build wealth, do it by purchasing real estate."* This section will focus on the emergence of government-backed programs that helped spark a huge construction boom after the Great Depression (1929-1933) that made homeownership possible for many Americans, more specifically, White Americans. We'll see how Jim Crow legislation (*structural layer*) affected the housing industry through the widespread use of restrictive covenants and a process called redlining. Additionally, fear and violence was used after the Civil War and through the mid-1900s to keep Blacks "in their place" in society by discouraging them from purchasing homes in White communities.

The Thomas Farmer case study was inspired by the story of my father, a Korean War Veteran. He married my mother, who was from an area near his hometown and they moved to California in pursuit of opportunity in the early 1950s. Upon arriving, his older brother guided and assisted him in finding a nice location for him to start a family. It wasn't until I got older and began looking for my first home a few years after graduating from college that I knew anything about the Federal Housing Authority (FHA). As my wife and I navigated the process, it dawned on me that my parents' journey to homeownership must've been a challenging one indeed.

The Federal Housing Authority was created by Congress in 1934 under the National Housing Act as a way to stimulate the construction industry, providing low down payment options for potential homeowners, and to improve home construction standards. This program made it possible for thousands of Americans to purchase a home, who would otherwise have to resort to the traditional ways of financing homes at the time which was making interest-only payments on a loan for a three to five year period, and at the end of the period, the homeowner had to pay the loan off in full or finance it again on similar terms as the previous loan.[16] With the FHA program, prospective homeowners could come up with a small down payment (opposed to 50%) and the FHA would insure the mortgage under their program in case the homeowner defaulted on the loan. So, basically the FHA is an insurance program that is funded by the premiums that homeowners pay to insure mortgages and it is backed by the government. According to a Washington Post article in 2013, the FHA has only needed taxpayers' support once in its history.[17] Let's take a look at how it works.

Here is an illustration ⟶

Before the FHA

Year 1

Loan amount: $5,000

Interest-Only, 5-year Term

Year 5

Loan balance: $5,000

Purchase price:	$10,000
Down payment:	$5,000
Loan amount:	$5,000

With the FHA

Year 1

Loan Amount: $9,500

Self-Amortizing, 20-year Term

Year 5

Loan Amount: $8,290

Purchase price:	$10,000
Down payment:	$500
Loan amount:	$9,500

The two examples illustrate the FHA's impact on home financing. In the first example, the buyer had to put 50% of the property's value down in order to meet the guidelines of a typical bank in the 1930s and 1940s. The loan was interest only, meaning that none of the monthly payments went to the principal amount borrowed. At the end of the three or five year period, the buyer was left with two options. They could pay off the full amount owed, which was the original loan amount, or they could finance the property again under similar terms. The FHA program totally revolutionized the home buying process by allowing buyers to purchase a home with a much lower down payment amount, lower interest rates, and for the first time, a self-amortized mortgage. I know that last benefit might be a little confusing, but here's what it means: the word 'mortgage' comes from the word *mortuus,* which simply means "dead"and Old French words *mort* (dead) and *gage* (pledge). Simply put, a mortgage is a pledge to death. Don't take that literally. We are talking about the loan itself, because it dies off over the course of the loan term. When we say the loan is "self-amortizing", we are essentially saying your monthly payments will decrease the loan amount over time.

In the second example, the home buyer only put down $500 instead of $5,000. This is huge because it was more realistic to come up with $500 instead of $5,000, especially in the 1930s after the Great Depression. I arbitrarily chose an 8% interest rate over 20 years with a loan amount of $9,500. At the 5-year point, the loan balance is now at $8,290. I used an amortization calculator to figure this out. You can search the Internet for an amortization table to input the same figures. After 20 years, the loan will be paid off.

Activity #5: Internet Search

Conduct an Internet Search
(Write down notes for each)

1. What percentage of people in the country owned homes versus renting homes at the time the FHA was created?

2. From 1934 to the mid-1960s, who did FHA benefit the most?

3. How did FHA go about benefiting a particular group?

There is no doubt FHA benefited Whites more than any other group. According to George Lipsitz, FHA and VA financed over a $100 billion worth of housing between 1934 and 1962, and 98% of these funds went to White families.[18] The efforts to maintain the power imbalance were deliberate and contributed to a huge wealth gap.

In order to fully grasp the social climate of the Jim Crow era, it's necessary to go back to the period immediately following the Civil War called Reconstruction. This was a time when the country made an attempt to ease former Confederate states and formerly enslaved people into the new ways in which the country would function. During this time, many Blacks moved to various cities in the Midwest, West, and East to escape violent attacks from whites in the South and began to settle in urban areas. As Rothstein puts it, Blacks lived "relatively peacefully" during the time immediately following the war because of federal protection, but when the period came to a close at the end of the 1877 presidential election, there were several segregation laws passed that further stripped Blacks of their rights and placed them in a position of inferiority.[19] One of the biggest cases of this time was the landmark, Plessy versus Ferguson case. This ruling further cemented separation along racial lines and upheld the "separate but equal" doctrine, which was the idea that Blacks and Whites could have separate public accommodations as long as they were equal. This ruling made separation legal, allowing states and municipalities across the country to enact laws and ordinances which openly discriminate against Blacks.

During the first quarter of the twentieth century, many cities and counties across the United States adopted sundown laws, also called sunset laws. They posted signs and sent threatening messages that Black were not to be in these towns when the sun goes down. This negative sentiment wasn't taken lightly. Many Black families were violently attacked by mobs, and there were even instances when whole towns occupied by Blacks were burned down. For instance, when several Black sharecroppers from Elaine, Arkansas, reached out to a White attorney from a nearby town to assist them in pressing for fair treatment from a local landowner, the meeting at a local church in Elaine resulted in shots being fired into the church.[20] The Black men returned fire and a White man was killed. Mobs of White men massacred about 200 Blacks, while 5 Whites were killed in total.

This level of terror made Blacks fearful of entering White communities. In addition to the threat of physical harm, there were also policies passed by local municipalities, some directly backed by government programs such as the FHA, that also kept communities racially segregated. The FHA and VA were involved in a process called *redlining*. Redlining is a practice that denies loans to people usually based on the person's race, where they live, or where they want to live. This practice was prevalent during the Jim Crow era and was used to segregate communities throughout the country. In Richard Rothstein's masterful work, *The Color of Law*, he takes a deep dive into explicit policies at all levels of government that set the stage for racial discrimination in housing. One of the ways the FHA used redlining against non-White groups was using colored maps like the one you see here of Los Angeles in 1939:

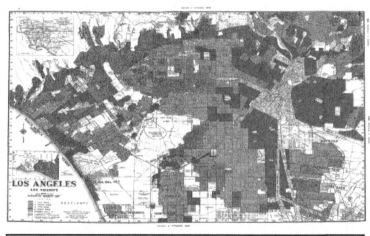

| Grade A - Most Desirable |
| Grade B -Desirable |
| Grade C -Declining |
| Grade D - Undesirable |

As a result of this governmental practice, many Blacks and other non-Whites were not able to take advantage of the FHA and VA low interest, government-backed loan programs. This, along with other discriminatory practices, made it difficult for Blacks to purchase homes in certain areas, forcing them into densely populated urban areas while Whites enjoyed the benefits of government-backed loans in surrounding suburbs.

Restrictive Covenants

Many White property owners discriminated against Blacks through the use of restrictive covenants on property deeds. A property deed is basically an agreement that transfers ownership of a piece of real estate from one person to another. A restrictive covenant is a legal agreement written into to the deed of a property that lists specific obligations that the purchaser of the property must adhere to.[21] They were created for Whites to maintain communities where only Whites lived, claiming that this would allow them to maintain high home values in their communities. Because it was difficult for neighbors in a White community to sue if a White neighbor sold to a non-White family, many communities sought to get around this by getting the neighbors sign the deed, restricting the sale to a non-White person. When these weren't effective, the owners tried another method by forming associations to keep non-Whites out.[22] Many of these covenants were enforceable until the Shelly versus Kraemer case of 1948, a landmark Supreme Court case, that put an end to racially restrictive covenants. The Court decided unanimously that state enforcement of restrictive covenants violated the Equal Protection Clause of the 14th Amendment. Thurgood Marshall and the great Loren Miller argued that case and won.

Activity #6: Internet Search and Analyze (Group or Individual)

In this activity, you will conduct an Internet search on **Restrictive Covenants**. After you conduct the search, you will take notes on what you find and answer the questions below.

1. Refer back to your responses on page 88 regarding *restrictive covenants.* Go back to the web page and jot down one of the lines that specifically addressed restrictive covenants in any of the documents.

2. In what ways did the structural and ideologocal layers of racism influence the real estate industry (and the economy) after the Great Depression?

3. What long-term effects do you think redlining had on communities throughout the United States?

4. What long-term implications do you think redlining had on the net worth of the average White family versus a Black family?

We covered some of the effects that legalized segregation had on Blacks in this country. From the convict leasing system that pushed many Blacks back into servitude, to governmental practices that backed racial segregation in housing, to restrictive covenants that prevented Blacks and other non-Whites from purchasing homes in areas occupied by Whites. All of these things have had long-term effects on the lives of Blacks and other non-White people. Many of these inequities are still operating in our daily social interactions, deeply rooted in policies and practices, and we must continue to be vigilant in our commitment to dismantling these systems of inequity in order to create a more equitable world.

Books/Websites to Check Out		
Title	Author/Website	Type
The Color of Money	Richard Rothstein	Book
The Federal Housing Administration	https://www.hud.gov/program_offices/housing/fha-history	Website

Helping Mrs. Hanson with her Concerns

Before revisiting the case study, use the **TREC Method** to help guide your response to Keila. You will be playing the role of her counselor, Mrs. Hanson. If you need to, please go back to the script at the beginning of the chapter and read through it before going to the next section.

Using the TREC Method to address the dilemma

What should Mrs. Hanson be thinking about?

THINK:

How can Mrs. Hanson ensure she shows respect as she tries to address the problem?

RESPECT:

How can Mrs. Hanson demonstrate empathy for Keila in this dilemma?

EMPATHY:

What are some ways in which Mrs. Hanson might show compassion by helping Keila?

COMPASSION:

"Why can't I just take the African American Literature class?"

"I mean, it might be fun. I've never actually taken a class on anything dealing with Africa before."

"What should I do?"

CHAPTER 4 CHECKUP

1. Institutional racism works in isolation. It is not informed by ideological racism nor is it situated within structures of racism.

True ☐   False ☐

2. Which of the following are ways institutional racism might operate in our country?

    ☐ within educational systems
    ☐ within industries
    ☐ court rulings
    ☐ at the individual level

3. The convict lease system was put into place after the Civil War and used to force many formerly enslaved people back into a legal form of servitude.

True ☐   False ☐

4. What is the difference between structural racism and institutional racism?

5. Explain how the FHA violated the rights of non-Whites groups from 1934 to the end of the Civil Rights era.

DEAR MRS. PRINCIPAL ACTIVITY

After meeting with Mrs. Hanson, Keila sends her this text message:

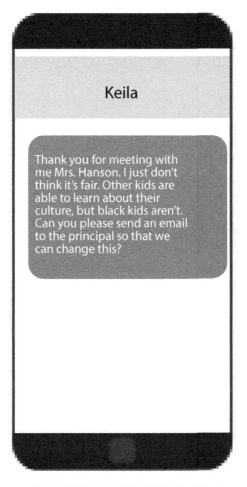

Keila

Thank you for meeting with me Mrs. Hanson. I just don't think it's fair. Other kids are able to learn about their culture, but black kids aren't. Can you please send an email to the principal so that we can change this?

In an effort to help Keila and other Black students at her school, Mrs. Hanson has decided to write the principal an email message. Mrs. Hanson calls you and asks for specific things to include in the message. She wants to make sure says the right things and understands how complex racism is. What bit of advice might you give Mrs. Hanson? Write a short email message to Mrs. Hanson on the next page.

Write a Sample Email Message Below

New Message

To: Mrs Hanson

Subject:

Send

Endnotes

1   Ibram X. Kendi, *How to be an Antiracist* (New York: Random House, 2019), 18.

2   Claude Anderson, *Powernomics: The National Plan to Empower Black America* (Maryland: PowerNomics Corporation, 2001), 5.

3   Ibid, 6.

4   Mehrsa Baradaran, "A Bad Check for Black America," Boston Review, August 8, 2018, https://www.bostonreview.net/class-inequality-race/mehrsa-baradaran-bad-check-black-america.

5   Patrick Sharkey, *Stuck in Place* (Chicago: University of Chicago Press, 2013), 2.

6   Julia B. Isaacs, "Economic Mobility of Black and White Families," Brookings (Brookings, July 28, 2016), https://www.brookings.edu/research/economic-mobility-of-black-and-white-families/.

7   Lisa J. Dettling et al., "Recent Trends in Wealth-Holding by Race and Ethnicity: Evidence from the Survey of Consumer Finances," The Fed - Recent Trends in Wealth-Holding by Race and Ethnicity: Evidence from the Survey of Consumer Finances, accessed August 22, 2021, https://doi.org/10.17016/2380-7172.2083.

8   "The Origins of Modern Day Policing," NAACP, May 9, 2021, https://naacp.org/find-resources/history-explained/origins-modern-day-policing.

9   Douglas A. Blackmon, *Slavery by Another Name* (New York: Anchor, 2008), 61.

10   "The 13th Amendment of the U.S. Constitution," National Constitution Center – The 13th Amendment of the U.S. Constitution, accessed August 22, 2021, https://constitutioncenter.org/interactive-constitution/amendment/amendment-xiii.

11   Robert Perkinson, *Tough Texas: The Rise of America's Prison Empire* (New York: Metropolitan Books, 2010), 105.

12   Douglas A. Blackmon, *Slavery by Another Name* (New York: Anchor, 2008).

13   Ibid, 69.

14   Matthew J. Mancini, *One Dies, Get Another: Convict Leasing in the American South, 1866-1928* (South Carolina: University of South Carolina Press, 1996), 1-2.

15   "Criminal Justice Fact Sheet," NAACP, May 24, 2021, https://www.naacp.org/criminal-justice-fact-sheet/.

16   "Federal Housing Administration: HUD.gov / U.S. Department of Housing and Urban Development (HUD)," Federal Housing Administration | HUD.gov / U.S. Department of Housing and Urban Development (HUD), accessed August 22, 2021, https://www.hud.gov/program_offices/housing/fhahistory.

17   Dina ElBoghdady, "FHA Needs $1.7 Billion Taxpayer Subsidy," The Washington Post (WP Company, September 27, 2013), https://www.washingtonpost.com/business/economy/fha-needs-17-billion-taxpayer-subsidy/2013/09/27/dd70ef90-276b-11e3-b3e9-d97fb087acd6_story.html.

18   George Lipsitz, *The Possessive Investment in Whiteness* (Philadelphia: Temple University Press), 1-2.

19   Richard Rothstein, *The Color of Law* (New York: Liveright, 2017), 78.

20   "The Massacre of Black Sharecroppers That Led the Supreme Court to Curb the Racial Disparities of the Justice System," Smithsonian.com (Smithsonian Institution, August 2, 2018), https://www.smithsonianmag.com/history/death-hundreds-elaine-massacre-led-supreme-court-take-major-step-toward-equal-justice-african-americans-180969863/.

21   Richard Rothstein, 79.

22   Ibid, 77-91.

Chapter 5

Cultural Racism

Social and cultural norms are influenced by the group in power.

The purpose of this chapter is to explore how the outer layers of racism (ideological, structural, and institutional) influence culture, and how messaging about the influencer culture projects onto others through various means.

- understand cultural racism and how it operates
- construct your own definition of cultural racism
- analyze and discuss how culture influences behaviors and practices
- recognize how cultural racism is operating in a life-like scenario and devise a plan on how to address it

- access to the Internet

Stereotypes
Microaggressions
Negatives perceptions
National beliefs   Social norms
Cultural representations
Media images
Implicit biases

Cultural Racism

Because the cultural norms and beliefs of the group in power are viewed as 'normal', everything else is judged against it, whether it's the way you talk, walk, look, learn - every single thing.

Introduction: Cultural Racism

Whereas structural racism functions in the big frameworks where institutions are situated, the cultural layer of racism looks more at the norms, beliefs, and practices of the influencer culture and how they are normalized and reinforced through sources such as the media, entertainment, textbooks, communication, and many others. This layer is constantly informed by the ideological layer and insulated within structures and institutions where it gives the group with the most power advantages that are not afforded to other groups.

In this chapter, we will be exploring cultural racism through discussions, reflecting on cultural norming, and analyzing two case studies where you will be identifying how cultural racism might be operating. You will finish by applying the TREC Model to a life-like scenario and think about how you could address cultural racism when you see it.

Cultural racism is dangerous because it consists of norms, shared beliefs, and practices that reinforce racial stereotypes.

■　■　■

Mrs. Sanders is a first-year kindergarten teacher in a diverse school district. She was excited when hired in her first interview and eager to get started working on decorating her classroom for the upcoming school year. In her first meeting with the administrative staff, they conveyed to her the importance of making sure every child is given equal access to resources and that their individual needs are met. This was no problem for Mrs. Sanders, she was well versed in State

Education Code and knew all of the laws regarding how to support children in the classroom, especially students from diverse backgrounds.

Her first week of school went well. She was happy to report to the principal that her kids were able to identify colors, shapes, and numbers. They made so much progress towards their goals during the first quarter that Mrs. Sanders was recognized at

one of the staff meetings for her great work. Though she was a little nervous prior to standing in front of the staff and sharing a few bits about her experiences, she was proud of herself because she accepted that talking in front of crowds had always been a problem for her.

On one afternoon, Principal Vincent received a phone call from a parent. The parent was upset that her son expressed that he had a bad day and was sad. Based on the parent's account, this was because "Mrs. Sanders read a book and none of the children in the book looked like his son." The parent's frustration was even more upsetting since he had volunteered to be on the school's Diversity Committee the previous school year, but had yet to receive a call from school's staff. The parent's exact words were, "I thought I was doing the right thing by signing up because I know there are very few Black teachers at the school."

The parent also told the principal that he called Mrs. Sanders to share what his son had told him about feeling "left out" during class. Mrs. Sanders' response was, "Well, the images in the books are just normal kids. I'm not sure what the problem is." The parent became more enraged and told Mrs. Sanders he would be calling the principal.

The principal listened intently and expressed her apologies for what happened. First, she took responsibility for not reaching out to parents who volunteered to be on the Diversity Committee with the excuse that it was an accreditation year and much of the staff's time was used to plan for the upcoming visit.

Activity #1: Discuss in Groups (or as an individual reflection)

1. What inequities do you think might be operating in this case?

2. What is the main dilemma in this case? What do you see?

3. What opportunities are there to remove any inequities presented in this case?

4. If you were in Mrs. Sander's position, what would you do?

5. What is the principal's role in this and what can she do to resolve the issue?

Activity #2: Analyzing Inequity

6.

1. What forms of racism might be operating here? Write down evidence.

	Layer	Evidence
☐	Ideological	
☐	Structural	
☐	Institutional	
☐	Cultural	
☐	Interpersonal	

Culture and the Media

Cultural racism is dangerous because it consists of norms, shared beliefs (schemas), and practices that reinforce racial stereotypes that are informed by racist ideology and play out in the world through basic social interactions, and implicit biases. One of the main conduits for this messaging is the media.

As a kid, I remember watching what we called "Cowboy and Indian" movies with my brothers. I particularly liked watching John Wayne films. He was tall, powerful, and always seemed to make the right decisions to get himself out of a tight bind. In the end, no matter how difficult the challenge, he was sure to come out on top. I also liked watching the Rifleman with Chuck Connors. He was always cool and collected, never sweating, and would always find a way out of a dilemma because he could use his rifle to take down the toughest outlaw. Or the Big Valley, one of the most successful dramatic series of all time. Victoria Barkley, played by Barbara Stanwyck, the bright and elegant matriarch with three amazing sons, Heath, Jarrod, and Nick, and her daughter, Audra. They were rich, owned a huge ranch in Stockton, CA., they

were fair, upstanding, model citizens in a sometimes corrupt world that tested them as a family. Or, what about Big Hoss and his brothers Little Joe and Adam, and their father Ben, known as the Cartwrights. If I could calculate the number of hours I spent watching these shows and others like them, I believe the total would be somewhere in the thousands.

Like many other kids growing up in America during my time, we were fans of Westerns. When playing with my friends or cousins, I always wanted to be a Cowboy, never an "Indian" (we used this term to refer to Native Americans). One of the toys we played with as kids was a cap gun. They had these nicely crafted die cast metal designs that looked and felt like real guns, and they came with paper cap strips that had to be pushed inside of the gun so when you pulled the trigger, the hammer came slamming down on the strip and you would hear a *pop*. This was a lot of fun. Some of the cap guns even came with holsters that you could wrap around your waist just like your favorite movie star. But, what I didn't know, or didn't even realize, was how much I had been conditioned to think of White men as powerful, and how much I associated them with guns. With all of the negative imagery we had seen, and hearing derogatory phrases such as "Indian-giver", none of us chose to be Indians that often.

I agree with George Lipsitz's take on this dilemma. He describes "Whiteness" as only an abstraction in law, but it plays out in our social world by "uniting ethnically diverse European audiences into an imagined community -- one called into being through inscribed appeals to the solidarity of White supremacy."[1] Media representations play a significant role in shaping ideas and forming meaning to racial identity, and these attitudes and behaviors are played out in social contexts.

Activity #3: Reflection (Personal)

Read the questions below and answer in the space provided.

1. What do you think my brain has stored about these men?

2. If you have ever seen these shows or shows similar to them, have you developed similar perceptions?

3. What unconscious beliefs do you think are operating here?

4. What other derogatory colloquialisms have you heard about Native Americans or another group based on what you have seen through the media?

5. What can we do to change this? (we will address more of this later)

It's Just a Black Face to You, But Not to Me

As a college student I had the privilege of being a part of a pretty tight-knit Black community, though I attended a predominately White university. The school's enrollment was in the neighborhood of 24,000, and around 600 to 700 students were African American, with the biggest segment of this group likely being student-athletes. I was fortunate to be a college athlete on a full-scholarship, made friends on the team and outside of the team, and felt accepted in the community. I also joined a Black fraternity and was active in the Black Student Union, which became the African Student Alliance in my sophomore year.

Everything appeared to be going quite well during my first two years, even though there were a few racial incidents that we had to work through. The one that I remember most vividly was when a group of White students dressed up like Aunt Jemima characters and did a rendition of *Salt-N-Pepa's* popular song *Push It*. We were enraged, which is a natural response to such foolish behavior. A lot of people took it as a joke and thought we should "pay it no mind", but it was unsettling knowing that we attended school with people who didn't understand that performing such blatant satirical acts painted negative views of people across cultural lines and is flat out dehumanizing. We sought an explanation through school leadership and they said they would handle it.

I'm not sure of the outcome of our complaining and bringing awareness to school leadership, but what I do know, is it made us much more aware of how deep racism ran in institutions and what we needed to do to dismantle it. For instance, when the newly renovated University Center was completed with new banquet-style rooms and conference rooms, my fraternity was one of the first groups to request one of the rooms for a dance. The receptionists were not pleased when we refused to turn away from their ridiculous requests in order to rent space. We came back every few days until they finally let us talk to someone who was also Black, and he gave us the rundown on how to go about renting space for dances. A few weeks later, we reserved the room and had a dance in the new facility. This speaks to the power of having allies who can help you navigate social settings. It's upsetting to know that racism still exists and is continuing to manifest itself culturally. As recently as 2019, there are still racial incidents such as the posting of the N-word on social media by a member of a predominately White fraternity when promoting a philanthropic event, according to the October 2019 article published in the school's newspaper.[2] This is in no way bashing the university. They have taken intentional steps to create a more inclusive environment, but this speaks more to the need for more comprehensive education on cultural awareness for everyone.

If identifying derogatory colloquialisms and making a personal commitment to not using them could solve the issues stemming from cultural racism, then dismantling racism might seem like a simple task, but it's not. Racism runs deep and affects all areas of human activity and manifests in beliefs, attitudes, and behaviors that have resulted in violenct acts towards others. These attitudes will continue to result in violence and unconscionable acts of terror against people of color throughout our society if we allow these behaviors to go undetected and normalized. Ideology constantly feeds culture and it is important that we understand how they are interlinked. There's a common perspective that racism doesn't exist unless it is an explicit law, policy, rule, or action by an individual. That's simply not true, it's everywhere.

In the next section, we will explore a popular Ice Cream truck song that I've heard since I was a kid. The song might trigger feelings of uneasiness, and that's not my intention. I'm sharing this song simply because I think we need to be vigilant when addressing unfairness, and often, it's not so blatant.

Popsicles on a Hot Summer Day

Like many kids, I loved hearing the sweet sounds of the ice cream truck's tunes drifting through the air on a hot summer day. I remember digging deep into my pockets and hoping to feel the cool touch of coins as I wiggled my fingers vigorously.

If I didn't feel any change, I would dart into the house in search of a few silver coins, in drawers, on my nightstand, and if I was really desperate, I would flip the pillows on our couch. I was certain to find some change there, along with afro picks (K Cutters), a few popcorn kernels, and maybe a Snicker bar wrapper.

But, what never dawned on me, is one of the well known tunes that I've heard thousands of times was not a children's song at all. Check out the lyrics to the song on the next page:

Cultural racism is dangerous because it consists of norms, shared beliefs (schemas), and practices that reinforce racial stereotypes that are informed by racist ideology and play out in the world through basic social interactions, and implicit biases. One of the main conduits for this messaging is the media.

N***** Want a Watermelon Ha! Ha! Ha! Ha!

"singer: "hold up jackson! time to cut a watermelon. you n****** quit throwin' them bones and come down and get your ice cream!"

black men: "ice cream?"

singer: "yes. ice cream! colored man's ice cream. watermelon!"

well i went down to coonville the other afternoon
there i saw a yella girl her name was susie loon
she was sitting on a rail with the fields to her back
eating watermelon to make the n**** fat
she says i'm susie dear would you give your heart to me
i can keep a hundred boys busy don't you see
the juice from the watermelon trickled down her chin
i said if ya give me a hundred i will tell ya like this

n**** love a watermelon ha, ha, ha, ha!
n**** love a watermelon ha, ha, ha, ha!
for here, they're made with a half a pound of co'l
there's nothing like a watermelon for a hungry coon

n**** love a watermelon ha, ha, ha, ha!
n**** love a watermelon ha, ha, ha, ha!
for here, they're made with a half a pound of co'l
there's nothing like a watermelon for a hungry coon
well the watermelon grows on a big green vine
and when the n**** sees them he takes them by the five

he knows which ones are ripe with a great big whack
they go bum bum when you hit them on the back
the best way to get them is to steal them if you can
if you don't want to steal them you get a colored man
take him to your house and you give him to your wife
then you mark him on the back with the nick of a knife

n**** love a watermelon ha, ha, ha, ha!
n**** love a watermelon ha, ha, ha, ha!
for here, they're made with a half a pound of co'l
there's nothing like a watermelon for a hungry coon

n**** love a watermelon ha, ha, ha, ha!
n**** love a watermelon ha, ha, ha, ha!
for here, they're made with a half a pound of co'l
there's nothing like a watermelon for a hungry coon

well the n**** loves a possum and the n**** loves gin
the n**** loves a yella girl the n**** loves sin
the n**** loves to dance when it hears the banjo ring
but it goes for the watermelon very first thing
the coon was made for the melon that grows
the watermelon was made for the colored man too
put them on on the alter and you all will agree
the n**** was made for the watermelon and melon for he
n**** love a watermelon ha, ha, ha, ha!
n**** love a watermelon ha, ha, ha, ha!
hit the banjo and we will have another tune
there's nothing like a watermelon for a hungry coon".

Link to Video

 https://youtu.be/1x6RcYxDc7s

If the link above is no longer active, conduct an Internet search and see if you can find it. If not, I have posted the lyrics above.

"N***** Want a Watermelon Ha! Ha! Ha!Ha" was performed by Harry C. Browne and released in 1916 by Columbia Records. Browne used the same melody from a well known song created in the 19th century that was often used in minstrel shows called *Turkey in the Straw*, where White actors and performers dressed up and painted their face black.[4] It's difficult to hear and watch, but necessary to understand the damage that songs like this have caused Black people over the years.

Activity #4: Reflection (Group or Individual)

Read the lyrics to the song in this section or watch the video. Please see the link above to the video clip.

1. What is your general reaction to the song?

2. Have you heard this song before? Did you ever hear the lyrics?

3. How is racism operating in this song? Which layer(s) of racism?

4. Once the layer of racism is identified, what steps would you take to address the issue?

Mr. Garner Hears the Song

Mr. Garner is playing catch with his son and daughter when he hears musical tunes that can only come from an ice cream truck. At the same time, his kids jumps for joy and turn their heads swiftly in the direction of the tune. "Ooh, can we get an ice cream," Suji says, bubbling in excitement.

Mr. Garner smiles back at his two kids, touched by their antsy antics. "Of course. Let's get some ice cream."

"Yes," the kids chorus.

As Mr. Garner reaches into his back pocket for his wallet, he can't help but notice this is the same song that was discussed in a professional development training on his job. "It's the watermelon song," he thought to himself, "and this is the same truck I've seen for years."

Using the TREC Method to address the dilemma

What should Mr. Garner be thinking about?

THINK:

How can Mr. Garner ensure he shows respect as he tries to address the problem?

RESPECT:

How can Mr. Garner demonstrate empathy for the driver in this dilemma?

EMPATHY:

What are some ways in which Mr. Garner might show compassion?

COMPASSION:

As we see, cultural racism is buried deep in social and cultural norms and continuously informed by ideology. No one would ever think a song that is used to attract kids to an ice cream truck can be so dehumanizing. But, what's important here is that we develop strategies on how to identify it and get rid of it. The first step is to think about where the inequity is coming from, then think about how it is situated (from which layer is it operating), and then decide to make a respectful effort to change it. In the scenario above, it might be difficult to make broad changes to a complex issue such as this one. Do you think Mr. Garner's is done by simply influencing one person's decision to not play a specific tune on his/her ice cream truck? That's a tough question. Obviously, helping one person to respect the humanity of others is certainly better than not addressing the problem at all. But, what about other ice cream truck entrepreneurs? Who is responsible for regulating their line of business? Is there someone else who Mr. Garner should speak to in order to get the song deleted from all ice cream truck drivers' rotation? These questions make us dig deeper into the issue.

Here's another example of cultural racism. Take a look at this video. This video displays blatant racist ideas about Mexican people. It's hard to believe something like this even made it through marketing team discussions of a major brand between 1967 and 1971. When I see something as disgraceful as this, I wonder how much more disparaging imagery made it through media channels during those times. As you think about addressing racist messaging like this, it's always important to go through the process of identifying where the stereotype is operating first. This will inform you on what approaches are at your disposal to begin addressing the issue with the goal of eliminating it.

Frito Bandito Commercial

> 🔊 https://youtu.be/s9P-JjbDD6U

> *If the link above is no longer active, conduct an Internet search and see if you can find it. There are several commercials with the same character.*

As you are completing the **TREC Method,** think about how you might address the company that released this commercial. The TREC Method applies here too. Here's a thought:

"I want something to change. I'm going to put some thought into what the problem is and where it's coming from. I'm going to make an attempt to change it and respect those involved. I'm going to shift my perspective and put myself in their position (empathy). Lastly, I'm going to help them by offering a solution to the problem (compassion)."

Using the TREC Method to address the dilemma

What should you be thinking about?

THINK:

How can you ensure you show respect as you try to address the problem?

RESPECT:

How can you demonstrate empathy for others in this dilemma?

EMPATHY:

What are some ways in which you might show compassion?

COMPASSION:

Activity #5: Reflection (Group or Individual)

Conduct an Internet search and view the Frito Bandito Commercial. After viewing the video, answer the questions below. If the video is not available, see if you can find a transcript of the commercial.

1. What is your general reaction to the video?

2. Have you seen this video before? What are you wondering?

3. How is racism operating in this video? What layer(s) of racism?

4. Once the layer of racism is identified, what steps can be taken to address the stereotype?

5. What are some ways in which the stereotypes in the video have played out in the real world?

Read the story on the opposite page and answer the questions that follow.

After reading the Teacher Reprimand scene, answer the questions below. There are no right or wrong answers here.

1. What is the dilemma in this scenario?

2. What additional questions do you think the parents should ask?

3. Is some form of inequity operating in this scene? Please explain.

4. Once the layer is identified, what steps can be taken to address the issue?

Using the TREC Method to address the dilemma

What should you be thinking about?

THINK:

How can you ensure you show respect as you try to address the problem?

RESPECT:

How can you demonstrate empathy for others in this dilemma?

EMPATHY:

What are some ways in which you might show compassion?

COMPASSION:

CHAPTER 5 CHECKUP

1. Cultural racism is dangerous because it consists of norms, shared beliefs (schemas), and practices that reinforce racial stereotypes that are informed by racist ideology.

   True ☐   False ☐

2. Which of the following are ways cultural racism might operate in our country?

   ☐ within institutions
   ☐ within communities
   ☐ through the media
   ☐ within structures

3. One of the main ways in which cultural racism is presented is through the media.

   True ☐   False ☐

4. What is the relationship between ideological racism and cultural racism?

5. In what ways has the media reinforced racial stereotypes?

6. Write your own definition of **Cultural Racism.**

OFFENSIVE GROUP TEXT MESSAGE

Your company has an annual potluck. There is one Black person on your team and her name is Kimberly. Below is a group text message from one of your team members:

Group Message

Aye, why don't one of y'all tell Kimmy to bring some chitlins to the potluck. LOL!!!!!!!!!!!!!!!!

Your response to the text message below:

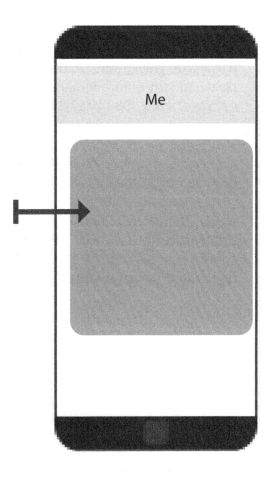

1. Is it important for you to respond to this message? If so, why?

2. Do you think you need to share this with someone outside of your group?

Endnotes

1   Lipsitz, 370.

2   Hosam Elattar, "Black Student Union Demands Change After Fraternity's Racial Slur," Daily Titan, October 22, 2019, https://dailytitan.com/news/campus/black-student-union-demands-change-after-fraternity-s-racial-slur/article_e212a9c7-c8f9-5908-baa2-39c9cb6cb0d6.html.

3   Harry C. Browne, "N***** Love a Watermelon, HA! HA! Ha! Lyrics," azlyrics.biz, accessed September 22, 2021, https://azlyrics.biz/h/harry-c-browne-lyrics/harry-c-browne-nigger-love-a-watermelon-ha-ha-ha-lyrics/.

4   Theodore R. Johnson, "Recall That Ice Cream Truck Song? We Have Unpleasant News for You," NPR (NPR, May 11, 2014), https://www.npr.org/sections/codeswitch/2014/05/11/310708342/recall-that-ice-cream-truck-song-we-have-unpleasant-news-for-you.

Chapter 6
Interpersonal Racism

Individual racist beliefs, biases, or acts towards another group or person.

The purpose of this chapter is to examine racism at the interpersonal level and look at how racist ideological, structural, institutional, and cultural racism, inform individuals and affect interpersonal interactions.

...what you will be able to do at the end of this chapter:

- understand interpersonal racism and how it operates
- construct your own definition of interpersonal racism
- analyze statistical outcomes and discuss how cultural racism informs and influences interpersonal interactions
- work cooperatively with others to gain a better understanding and different perspectives on interpersonal racism
- analyze how individual racism is operating in a life-like scenario and devise a plan to address it

...materials needed for this chapter:

- access to the Internet

Hate crimes

Racial slurs

Physical violence

Hate speech

Racial bias

Emotional violence

Discrimination

Interpersonal Racism

Social interactions are influenced by various things such as cultural norms, beliefs, policies, and stereotypes, to name a few.

Introduction: Interpersonal Racism

As we have learned so far, racism is a layered system that functions in a continuous loop, where the ideology and culture inform individuals and influence social interactions, within structures and institutions. When we think of racism at the interpersonal layer, we want to think about the individual acts of hatred, discrimination, or violence inflicted on others that might cause physical or emotional harm, whether it was intended or not. The distinction I want to draw from the other layers covered is that interpersonal racism is typically overt. We can see it on television, or read about it in a newspaper, or we might experience it personally. This is quite different from the other forms of racism that we have covered so far.

"Interpersonal racism typically occurs when an individual discriminates against someone else based on their racial group membership."

In this chapter, we will be reviewing historical facts and examining stories where you will have an opportunity to reflect, think, and apply your knowledge in a life-like simulation using the TREC Method.

■   ■   ■

The following is an excerpt from an audio recording transcript of Fountain Hughes in 1949. He was enslaved as a young kid and he recounts how life was for him while he was enslaved, and how things were when he was freed. The recording is archived in the Library of Congress under the title *Voices from the Days of Slavery: Stories, Songs, and Memories - Fountain Hughes (transcript):*

At the time of the recording, Fountain Hughes was 101 years old. He was interviewed by Hermond Norwood. When asked who he worked for as an enslaved person, here were some of Fountain Hughes responses:

> "Well, I belonged to the Burness when I was a slave. My mother belonged to Burness. But, we was all slave children and...soon after we found out we was free, why then, we was...bound out to other people...and all such people as that. And we would run away, and wouldn't stay with them. Why then, we'd just go and stay anywhere we could. Lay out at night anywhere. We had no home, you know. We was just turned out like a lot of cattle. You know how they turn cattle out in the pasture? Well, after freedom, you know, colored people didn't have nothing. Colored people didn't have no beds when they was slaves. We always slept on the floor, pallet here, and a pallet there just like...a lot...of wild people, we didn't...we didn't know nothing. They didn't allow us to look at no book."

> "We were slaves. We belonged to people. They'd sell us like they sell horses and cows and hogs and all like that. Have an auction bench, and they'd put you on...up on the bench and bid on you just the same as you bidding on cattle, you know."[1]

Hermond Norwood then asked how things were when he was enslaved and here were a few things Fountain Hughes shared:

> "...if you was bad and mean they didn't want to beat you and knock you around, they'd sell you."

> "They'd have a regular sale every month, you know, at the courthouse. And then they'd sell you, and get two hundred...hundred dollar...five hundred dollar."[2]

I encourage you to read the entire transcript or listen to the audio. It really gives you great insight on what life was like for African people who were enslaved here in the United States. Links to the audio and the transcript are below:

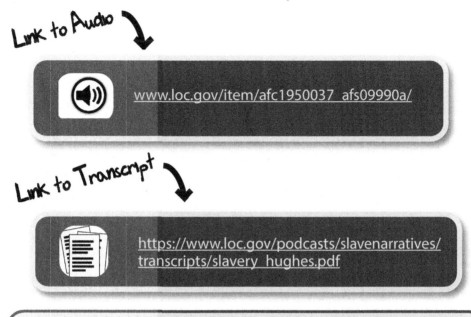

Link to Audio

www.loc.gov/item/afc1950037_afs09990a/

Link to Transcript

https://www.loc.gov/podcasts/slavenarratives/transcripts/slavery_hughes.pdf

If the links above are no longer active, conduct an Internet search and see if you can find the audio or the transcript of the interview.

Fountain Hughes' story is like many stories of Africans who left the plantation after slavery ended and found themselves still trapped in the vestiges of a dreadful past, only to find themselves facing more sophisticated forms of oppression. As we have seen throughout this book, racism is a deeply entrenched system that required careful and thorough examination to fully understand.

Before we jump into interpersonal racism more, let's reflect on Fountain Hughes' interview.

Read the excerpts from Fountain Hughes' interview again. Highlight or underline all signs of racism based on what he says, then copy the text in one of the five areas below where it fits most appropriately based on what we've learned thus far about the different layers of racism.

Activity #1: Name the Layer

Interpersonal Racism

_____

Cultural Racism

_____

Institutional Racism

_____

Structural Racism

_____

Ideological Racism

_____

Activity #2: Reflection (Group or Individual)

Read the transcript or listen to the audio and answer each question below. If the link is not active, please conduct an Internet search on "Fountain Hughes Interview."

1. Describe how the layers of racism are operating in Fountain Hughes' life?

2. What evidence from his interview supports the notion that ideology is informing other layers of racism?

3. What would you say if someone made the following statement, "Racism ended when slavery ended."

4. What are you wondering?

Interpersonal Racism in Action

Interpersonal racism typically occurs when an individual or group of individuals discriminate against someone else based on their racial group membership. This might happen when someone refuses to hire another person because of their race, denies leasing applications for housing, uses hate speech, language, or messaging, acts of violence, or a host of other actions that harm others. We might even see interpersonal racism operating in a company's hiring departments when the names of applicants who appear to be from any of the non-White groups are thrown out, or on school sites when teachers refer a high number of students from non-White categories to the office for discipline. These are a few examples of when we might see racism rear its ugly head and we are forced to respond in some way. For most people, interpersonal racism doesn't flash on their personal radar unless it's a blatant act, like being called the N-word, which I was once called by a woman in a department store. Or, maybe the time when my nephew and I were helping my sister move into her new apartment for seniors and one of the residents asked us, "Why are you here?"

To touch on the N-word (derogatory word used to reference Blacks) for moment, it's one of the most offensive words in the English language. This word has been used to degrade and dehumanize Africans for centuries. To quantify its toxic use against African people, author Randall Kennedy's 2001 research of federal and state court records revealed that the N-word appeared in 4,219 cases, compared to racial epithets used against other groups: "H-word" (Whites - 286), "G-word" (Asians - 90), "K-word" (Jews - 84), and "W-word" (Hispanics - 50).[3] So, if there was a racial epithet mentioned in a state or federal case, there's an 89.2% chance it would have been the N-word. Take a look at the chart on the next page.

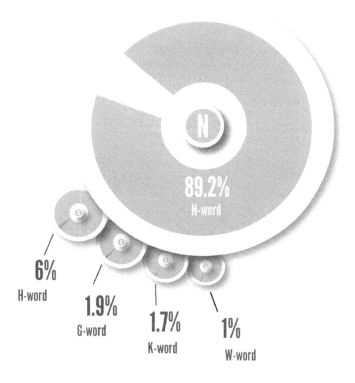

89.2%
N-word

6%
H-word

1.9%
G-word

1.7%
K-word

1%
W-word

What's important to remember about any acts of racism at the interpersonal level is the constant interplay between the ideological and cultural layers of racism and their influence on individual beliefs. Often, we think we can stop racism at the interpersonal level by reprimanding a person, firing them from their job, stop supporting them, or any other action used to deal with the individual and the behavior. This is an important step in correcting the behavior, but not the only step. What we often fail to see is how these individual acts are motivated by what has been socially normed. What I mean by this is that "race", as a political system, has created certain expectations and stereotypes based on how we have been categorized racially.

Activity #3: Personal Reflection (Group or Individual)

1. After viewing the data from the previous page, is there any piece of data that makes you wonder? Please share.

2. What is the data telling us?

3. What layer(s) of racism do you think are most influential in these outcomes?

4. What are some ways in which we can change these outcomes?

Four Boys

It was a typical sunny weekday afternoon and my friends Jonathan, Mason, Brandon, and I were walking down the narrow stretch of 135th Street in Compton near Stanford Avenue and Avalon Blvd, just before hitting McKinley Ave. We had just picked up some snacks from the local liquor store called Smitty's. We popped a few Now-Laters (yeah, that's how we pronounced it) into our mouths, guzzled down fruit punch from the tall plastic containers, and started flipping through the Los Angeles Times newspaper to review stats from Sunday's NFL games.

"Joe Cribbs had 140 yards rushing, what about Tony Dorsett? I bet he didn't even get a hundred," I sneered in Jonathan's direction, passing him the paper as we continued to stroll. Jonathan flipped through the paper, angled his head and tilted his chin into his chest to get a closer view of the paper.

"That's right boy!" Jonathan yelled, "Dorsett, one hundred and eighty-three homeboy. That's way more than Joe Cribbs. He prolly got like six hundred yards on the year and Dorsett is almost at a thousand, so you better talk that mess about Wendell Tyler 'cause it's all Cowboys on mine." Tim twisted his neck swiftly.

"Oh, you know Wendell Tyler got over a hundred, that's guaranteed -- every game." Jonathan looked to Mason.

"Check the stats," Jonathan added, giving the paper a push in Mason's direction. Mason snatched the paper and pulled it close to his face.

"He got over a hundred, like one-thirty something."

"That's alright," I snapped, "they still sorry and ain't gon' beat the Bills."

"Yeah right," Jonathan and Mason chorused.

We passed the Littleton's House on the corner of 135th and McKinley.

"Y'all smell that?" Brandon said, twisting his face into a sour expression.

"Ugh," the rest of us said in a quick succession.

This short two to three hundred yard stretch was always grungy, filled with the horrible scent of dog carcass mixed with garbage and lined with broken furniture that was obviously dumped by locals who always found 135th the right place to dump stuff. This was our typical walking route home. We lived about a mile and a half from the school in a tight-knit neighborhood on the western edge of Compton. Though none of us were gangbangers, we knew where we were from and knew how to handle ourselves if ever put in a predicament, and during the early 1980s, things were getting out of control with the increase in violence and the emergence of a new drug on the scene. We held our breaths and took brisk steps to get past the dead dog laying against the fence of the Brickyard. When we got a good distance away, Brandon turned his shoulders around and faced us.

"There go the boys, man." Startled, we kept walking down the straight path, trying not to make eye contact with the men in the black and white police car, as they reduced their speed and tracked us as we continued, shifting their heads in our direction.

"Where y'all going?" The 30ish, White male officer yelled through the opened window.

"We going home," we yelled back, in an irritated tone. We kept our heads and eyes straight as we walked. My heart danced around in my chest. After a few seconds, the engine revved up and the car skirted forward and then I heard the tires grinding into the gravel. Next, it came to a screeching halt with the front angled towards the sidewalk. We froze and turned in the car's direction. The two men exited the car. My heart pumped harder this time, thumping against the walls of my chest.

"Freeze right there," one of the officers grunted. We stood, speechless...and sucked wind through our teeth.

"Ain't nobody even doing nothing," I mumbled under my breath.

"Y'all got anything?" the tall cop asked.

"Naw." We all said, at nearly the same time.

"Well, you look suspicious," he said, eye-balling us all and stepping close to us. I shook my head and turned away from his piercing glare. "Why do you have an attitude?" he spouted, making his voice sound deeper than it really was.

"I don't have an attitude," I mumbled, tightening my lips against my teeth.

"Get your hands on the car." I took a deep sigh. His billy club dangled from his belt and he lowered his hand and gripped it. I took slow, careful steps to the car and then placed my hands on the hood, gently. I felt the heat of the hood and jerked back every so slightly. The next thing I knew, I was on the ground in a choke-hold. All I could think about is, "I hope my mother don't drive down this street and see me being choked-out by a police officer." She worked a few blocks away and drove down 135th to get to work daily.

Activity #4: Analyzing an Injustice

1. What forms of racism are operating here? Include evidence.

	Layer	Evidence
☐	Ideological	
☐	Structural	
☐	Institutional	
☐	Cultural	
☐	Interpersonal	

2. Read the **Visual** version of the Four Boys story to prepare for the next activity. This was a real experience that happened to me when I was 12 years old.

Activity #5: A Personal Story of Injustice

In this activity, you will be recalling a story **where you felt mistreated**. It can be a personal experience, something you heard or saw through some form of media, or an experience that someone else had that you are aware of.

Draw or sketch the story below using the panels provided. You can be as elaborate as you want or you can make it simple by drawing stick figures or faces. Use as many or as few of the panels as you need. Be sure to include speech bubbles in your panels. Use the Story Strip from the previous pages as a reference. Feel free to split the panels in halves. Dive into this project and use your creativity.

Story Title:

This incident was one of several encounters that I've had with the police throughout my life. It wasn't until I was able to research and examine what racism really is that I understood the nuances and subtleties which make it very difficult to detect, address, and dismantle. The worst part about many of these encounters, is that they usually result in internalizing the fear, feeling guilty or personally responsible for the encounter, and harboring feelings of powerlessness and hopelessness. My brain began to connect these experiences with perceptions of White men being powerful that I'd had seen thousands of times on television, and now connecting them with real life experiences.

Activity #6: Personal Reflection

1. How was your story similar or different from the Four Boys story?

2. Were there allies in your life who helped you get through situations like this? If so, please share.

Helping the Four Boys

The four boys in this case study were simply walking home from school, got questioned by law enforcement officers, and one was thrown to the ground and put into a chokehold. Not wanting to get his parents involved, how would you go about helping the kid deal with the matter if he came to you for advice? Please read through the case study once more before completing the **TREC Method**.

If you are in a group setting, you should form a small group and discuss the **TREC Method** before completing it. Of course, you can complete it independently as well.

Using the TREC Method to Address the Dilemma

What should you be thinking about?

THINK:

How can you ensure you show respect as you try to address the problem?

RESPECT:

How can you demonstrate empathy for others in this dilemma?

EMPATHY:

What are some ways in which you might show compassion?

COMPASSION:

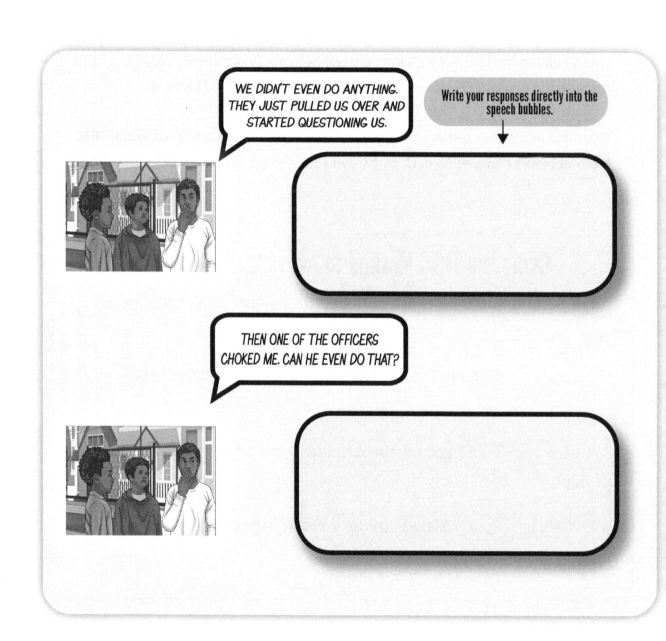

We will complete a short activity at the end of this chapter to tie up the **Four Boys** story. Remember, our goal is to focus on the story and see if there is a potential inequity operating. The inequity might be caused by racism, or it can be some other form of discrimination. The TREC Method is an easy way to view it through a critical lens to determine what's happening, who is being harmed, and steps we can take to change it.

CHAPTER 6 CHECKUP

1. Interpersonal racism occurs when a person from a group in power discriminates against someone from a group that lacks the same power.

    True ☐   False ☐

2. Which of the following are ways interpersonal racism might operate?
    - ☐ within institutions
    - ☐ within communities
    - ☐ while shopping in the store
    - ☐ when applying for a job

3. Interpersonal racism operates in normal settings where people interact.

    True ☐   False ☐

4. Why is it oftentimes difficult to dismantle racism at the interpersonal level?

5. Explain how racist ideology, structural, and institutional forms of racism, affect individuals or groups.

6. Write your own definition of **Interpersonal Racism.**

ADDRESSING THE MISCONDUCT

After talking to the four boys about the incident with the law enforcement officer, you are convinced that the boys are being completely honest and you would like to help.

With a few phone calls to acquaintances, you get additional information about the officer and find out there have been other complaints about his behavior.

Meet with your group and come up with four key steps in addressing the issue. Additionally, think of two "outer layer" (ideological, structural, institutional, cultural) ideas to address more broad issues. You can also work on this activity independently.

Notes

1

2

3

4

What are two ways to address outer layers here?

1

2

Endnotes

1   Hughes, Fountain, "Interview with Fountain Hughes, Baltimore, Maryland, June 11, 1949," The Library of Congress, accessed August 23, 2021, https://www.loc.gov/item/afc1950037_afs09990a/.

2   Ibid.

3   Gregory S. Parks and Shayne E. Jones, "N*****: A Critical Race Realist Analysis of the N-Word within Hate Crimes Law," https://scholarlycommons.law.northwestern.edu/ (98 Journal of Criminal Law and Criminology 1305, 2008), https://scholarlycommons.law.northwestern.edu/cgi/viewcontent.cgi?article=7306&context=jclc.

Chapter 7

Becoming Antiracist

Just as being racist requires action, so does being antiracist.

The purpose of this chapter is to put antiracist strategies into practice so that you can think of ways to identify racism when you see it and address it.

BECOMING

Racist

ANTIRACIST

...what you will be able to do at the end of this chapter:

- identify the different layers of racism
- recognize which layer, or layers, of racism is/are operating in a case study or life-like scenario
- develop a personal plan on how you will respond to racism when you see it operating
- create an infographic to inform others on what it means to be antiracist

...materials needed for this chapter:

- access to the Internet

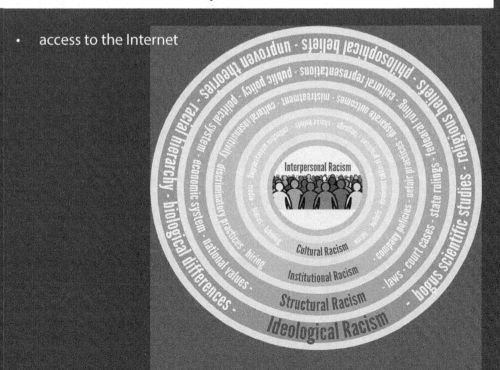

When you see an injustice, you have two choices. You can either pretend it doesn't exist and become complicit in its existence, or you can take action to change it. There's no neutral ground.

To Be or Not to Be an Antiracist

Over the last six chapters you have had the opportunity to explore the many facets of racism. It is my hope that the experience has been enlightening and given you some tools on how to approach race, and the system that operates continuously to separate people based on skin color, racism. As complex, deeply rooted, and entrenched the system is in inequity, and the massive damage it has caused humanity for over 500 years, I believe it can change. I believe the solutions lie within each of us, but we must be courageous and willing to conquer it and allow the beauty of all of humanity to flourish. This chapter is about the "doing". It's about taking action and **Becoming Antiracist**.

In this chapter, we will be exploring racism through two case studies and developing strategies on how to address similar acts of racism in real world contexts. You will be expected to refer back to the previous chapters and apply what you already know to each case study presented in this chapter. At the end of this chapter, you will be prepared to identify, address, and disrupt racism when you see it, hear about it, or experience it personally.

■   ■   ■

The struggle for universal freedom has been a long and enduring journey for many people in this country. The past has offered many clues on how to address injustice, and we have seen some changes take place at various levels of government, but there is still much work to be done. Before we dig into the case studies, I would like to remind you of some of the powerful voices in our country's past that might offer some motivation into the work we are about to embark on. These examples were carefully chosen, but please be encouraged to find others that represent the kind of action needed to disrupt and dismantle injustice so that the next chapter in the United States' history is better and more equitable than the last one.

In Activity #1, you will conduct an Internet search and gather information about individuals who took action against racism. It is important to learn about people who have taken steps to disrupt racism. I encourage you to find others. If you are in a group setting, each person should choose a person and after conducting research, you will have some dialogue on what you found. Complete at least three.

Activity #1: Internet Search

Frederick Douglas

1. What is this person known for?

2. What action or actions did this person take to disrupt racism or an inequity?

3. How has this person's action(s) helped humanity?

Activity #1: Internet Search

William Lloyd Garrison

1. What is this person known for?

2. What action or actions did this person take to disrupt racism or an inequity?

3. How has this person's action(s) helped humanity?

Activity #1: Internet Search

1. What is this person known for?

Angelina Grimke

2. What action or actions did this person take to disrupt racism or an inequity?

3. How has this person's action(s) helped humanity?

Activity #1: Internet Search

John Marshall Harlan

1. What is this person known for?

2. What action or actions did this person take to disrupt racism or an inequity?

3. How has this person's action(s) helped humanity?

Activity #1: Internet Search

Loren Miller

1. What is this person known for?

2. What action or actions did this person take to disrupt racism or an inequity?

3. How has this person's action(s) helped humanity?

Activity #1: Internet Search

Harriet Tubman

1. What is this person known for?

2. What action or actions did this person take to disrupt racism or an inequity?

3. How has this person's action(s) helped humanity?

Activity #2: Internet Search

In the next activity, conduct a search on the Internet and find two other individuals who took action to disrupt racism.

Name:

1. What is this person known for?

2. What action or actions did this person take to disrupt racism or an inequity?

3. How has this person's action(s) helped humanity?

Activity #2: Internet Search

Name:

1. What is this person known for?

2. What action or actions did this person take to disrupt racism or an inequity?

3. How has this person's action(s) helped humanity?

Activity #2: Internet Search

Name:

1. What is this person known for?

2. What action or actions did this person take to disrupt racism or an inequity?

3. How has this person's action(s) helped humanity?

Activity #3: Reflection (Group or Individual)

Now that you have conducted some research on individuals who have taken action against racism, form small groups to discuss your findings.

1. What did many of the people you researched have in common?

2. Discuss specific rights that they helped secure that we benefit from today.

3. Is racism operating more frequently in certain layers or do you see all five present throughout your analysis?

4. Name a specific action taken that disrupted some issue at the structural level? The institutional level?

5. How is ideology affecting each of the issues covered?

As you are reading through the case study, highlight or underline points where you might see an inequity, bias, or stereotype.

Mr. Carlo was ecstatic about his new teaching position with Imaginary School District. He was a recent graduate of Wordlow College, a small liberal arts school in Connecticut, and he decided to move to Dallas, TX, to start his career. He enrolled in the Beginning Teacher Support program and was excited to learn strategies on delivering powerful, engaging lessons. He was especially eager to open the minds of his young learners to the world of reading. He was hired in mid-Summer and given a 4th grade class consisting of many students new to the district. He adjusted to his new environment well and was encouraged by his new colleagues. During the professional development training just before the start of the school year, he was happy to find out that all of his books and materials arrived just in time.

A few weeks into the term, Mr. Carlo noticed that when there wasn't direct teaching or group work assigned, students became chatty and he had to continuously remind his students to return to their assigned seats. It had never dawned on him that students were racially segregated during these times and needed prompting to get back on task.

Mr. Carlo realized that 4th grade is an important stage in developing life-long literacy skills. Fourth grade is where the critical transition from 'learning to read' to 'reading to learn' takes place. He was trained on how to deliver a standards-based curriculum to build literacy and proficiency in the English Language Arts (ELA), and was provided additional support and guidance through the teacher support program. During an intensive summer in-service, he met with 3rd grade teachers during a collaborative Professional Learning Community (PLC) training, where they discussed what incoming 4th graders are expected to know. He found this to be invaluable because he had never taught before and was happy that other teachers were so willing to help. He expected students to be comfortable with language conventions, reading, decoding, basic text analysis, and they would have strong foundational writing skills. Veteran teachers reminded him that 4th grade readers will be reading more informational texts and required to analyze texts for facts and details that are essential to rich critical analyses. Mr. Carlo couldn't wait to examine texts with his students and was excited about the broad range of selections that his class would be covering. He was encouraged to scaffold and model lessons as often as needed and to differentiate when confronted with more difficult challenges. With the move to CA Common Core State Standards (CCSS) for ELA/Literacy, he didn't feel the anxiety that other teachers may have felt because he was a new teacher.

The first few weeks went quite well. Students were generally attentive, on task, and he used verbal/non-verbal prompts infrequently. One of the standards Mr. Carlo addressed first centered on getting students to understand that common values exist across different texts. Here, students had to analyze common story elements across various literary texts, draw connections, and make sense of how different genres share story elements. At the beginning of the lesson, he asked students to read a short excerpt from a story, identify key vocabulary words, and discuss guiding questions in small groups. Next, students read another literary text and conducted a critical analysis of both. One of the more covert themes addressed here is how different cultures share common lessons on life.

After a few weeks of class, Mr. Carlo realized that two African American boys began to talk during the literary text lesson. He calmly addressed both boys and gave them a referral for disrupting the class during instruction. This method of progressive discipline was used throughout the school. He was told by veteran teachers that "you want to get a handle on student behavior early." The boys didn't question the consequence, but felt they didn't deserve the detention. Mr. Carlo was quite disturbed because he treated all of his students with respect and didn't want them to think they could break classroom rules and get away without consequences. After thinking about it throughout the day, he decided to call one of the boy's parents. After probing over the phone for several minutes, trying to get a better *understanding as to why his behavior changed and why he chose not to serve the detention, one parent said, "He said your class is boring. And why can't you make the class more exciting for him."*

Mr. Carlo called each boy in during recess the next day to get a sense as to why they thought his class was boring. One of the boys said, "Those books are boring. All they talk about is White people." Mr. Carlo was speechless.

A few days later during a group reflection assignment, Mr. Carlo asked each group to present a short reflection to the class after reading a chapter in Charlie and the Chocolate Factory. Keith, one of the African American boys who had become somewhat detached from the lesson blurted out, "Man, this is stupid. Why we always reading this dumb stuff!" Several other students supported Keith's position with "Yeah. Why can't we read something else? Something that makes sense." Mr. Carlo quickly interjected, feeling that he needed to put an end to the disrespectful behavior.

"Now, that's enough class," he replied. "You are going to work on the assignment and not cause a disruption. This is a great book. It's part of your grade and you're going to read it without blurting out and making it difficult for the rest of the class."

The students could sense Mr. Carlo was upset. He was short and direct with his words for the rest of the period. During independent practice, Keith simply put his head down on the desk with the book dangling from his hand. Mr. Carlo noticed Keith's lack of interest in the activity, so he wrote another referral slip and placed it on the edge of Keith's desk. Keith sucked wind through his teeth and crumbled the small paper in his hand and let it fall to the floor. Mr. Carlo's heart thumped and he felt heat rising in his chest.

Recent Report from Imaginary School District

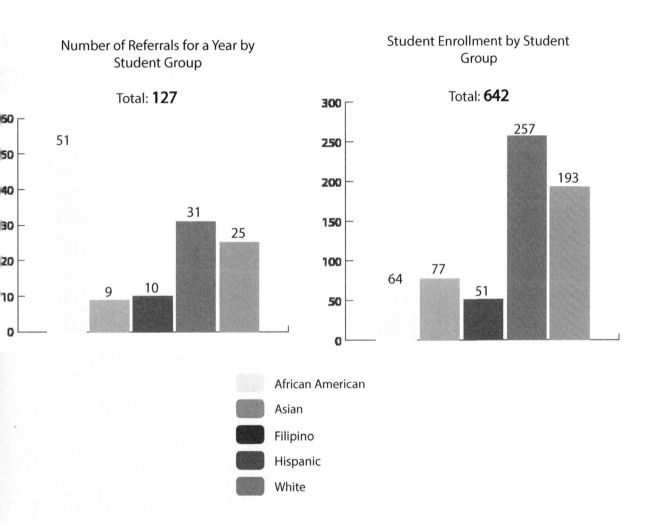

Number of Referrals for a Year by Student Group

Total: **127**

Student Enrollment by Student Group

Total: **642**

African American
Asian
Filipino
Hispanic
White

Racism Analysis Form

1. What forms of racism are operating in this case study? Write down evidence.

	Layer	Evidence
	Ideological	
	Structural	
	Institutional	
	Cultural	
	Interpersonal	

2. What does the data tell you about the student referral patterns at Imaginary School? Please use statistics here.

3. What additional questions might you have based on what the data is showing us?

4. What do you think is needed to disrupt the inequity operating in this case study?

Helping Mr. Carlo

There are many things to consider when examining this case study, from Mr. Carlo's inexperience, to being placed in a setting where there are already patterns working against a specific group of students. Mr. Carlo must respond to the several things operating that make this a challenging case.

I want you to pretend that you are a veteran teacher at Imaginary School and your principal requested that you meet with Mr. Carlo and start discussing a plan to address the issues. Consider everything you wrote on the Racism Analysis Form, and think about what you might recommend as a solution.

If you are in a group setting, you should form a small group and discuss the **TREC Method** before completing it

Activity #4: Discuss the TREC Method

Using the TREC Method to address the dilemma

THINK:	What should you be thinking about?
RESPECT:	How can you ensure you show respect as you try to address the problem?
EMPATHY:	How can you demonstrate empathy for others in this dilemma?
COMPASSION:	What are some ways in which you might show compassion by helping the teacher?

Plan for Disrupting a Potentia[

| Ideological Layer | What needs to change in this case? |
| | How do we change it? |

| Structural Layer | What needs to change in this case? |
| | How do we change it? |

| Institutional Layer | What needs to change in this case? |
| | How do we change it? |

| Cultural Layer | What needs to change in this case? |
| | How do we change it? |

| Individual Layer | What needs to change in this case? |
| | How do we change it? |

Inequity in Imaginary School District

In the space below, highlight the first (4) steps that you recommend the school takes to get rid of the potential inequity.

Steps:

①

②

③

④

Jacob, an assistant civil engineer for a medium size firm, had always aspired to be a senior civil engineer since his undergraduate days at a local university, where he excelled academically and was fortunate enough to get connected with a growing firm and landed his first internship. At his graduation, his supervisor, Linda, came to the ceremony and Jacob was ecstatic when she asked him if he'd like to join her team. "Of course," Jacob replied, with a gleaming smile. Jacob started working there just a few weeks after graduation and was intrigued by the resources and support the company offered to develop him as an engineer. On his first project he worked on a residential street improvement project and Jacob loved it. He thought to himself, "Not only am I able to get paid while doing what I love, I love the smile it puts on the faces of the people we help."

Soon, Jacob was assigned to other street improvement projects and began to really like working with his team. He was responsible for communicating with the construction team, overseeing much of the work, and built a good relationship with them. One afternoon, Jacob was inspecting slurry seal work that was recently completed and overheard two workers using racist epithets when referring to some of the residents in the area. This bothered Jacob. Not only because he was Hispanic and the hateful words were also referring to people of a common ethnicity, he simply felt it was wrong for anyone to use such horrible language towards other people.

Jacob became uneasy over the next two weeks and didn't quite know how to handle it. Because he was so new to the team, he didn't want to appear as if he couldn't handle some of the silliness that might come with the job. He talked to his friend about it and she encouraged him to speak to the workers about it. Jacob agreed that he'd let the first incident slide, "Maybe it's just me. They probably didn't mean any harm," he convinced himself. As the project progressed, Jacob heard additional slurs by the workers, and one afternoon he decided to address it by telling his supervisor. Linda was shocked by the news. She was genuinely empathetic and wanted to make sure Jacob felt safe and supported in his role. She told him she would handle it and Jacob trusted that she would.

The next day, Jacob discovered that the two workers were assigned to another project. Jacob didn't quite know how to feel. He was happy that the behavior was addressed, but he didn't feeling comfortable that the other workers didn't say much to him and he started to feel isolated. Over the next two weeks, Jacob started to think, "Maybe I shouldn't have said anything." But, he knew deep down inside he had to tell someone about the behavior.

Jacob completed the project and was assigned to many other similar projects over the next five years. He eventually purchased a home and started a family. His dreams of becoming a senior civil engineer were still fresh in his mind and he hoped to continue to do well in his current role. Another two years passed by and Jacob was still an assistant civil engineer with the firm. After training new engineers and watching them climb the ladder and become his supervisors, Jacob soon realized he was overlooked and knew he had to do something about it. It never dawned on him that he was the only Hispanic civil engineer with the firm and everyone else had been promoted, including Linda.

Racism Analysis Form

1. What forms of racism are operating in this case study? Write down evidence.

	Layer	Evidence
☐	Ideological	
☐	Structural	
☐	Institutional	
☐	Cultural	
☐	Interpersonal	

2. Discuss some of the challenges in this case.

3. What additional questions might you have based on what you know about this case?

4. What do you think is needed to disrupt the inequity in this case study?

Helping Jacob

There are many things to consider when examining this case study. From what we know, Jacob is a qualified engineer who has done great work with the firm.

I want you to pretend that you are Linda in this case and Jacob's new supervisor called you because he believes Jacob's motivation to work has diminished. Consider everything you wrote on the Racism Analysis Form, and think about what you might recommend as a solution.

If you are in a group setting, you should form a small group and discuss the TREC Method before completing it.

Activity #5: Discuss the TREC Guide

Using the TREC Method to address the dilemma

THINK: What should you be thinking about?

RESPECT: How can you ensure you show respect as you try to address the problem?

EMPATHY: How can you demonstrate empathy for others in this dilemma?

COMPASSION: What are some ways in which you might show compassion by helping the company?

Plan for Disrupting a Potentia

Only address the layer(s) involved in this case. If the layer isn't operating, mark the box with an "X".

| Ideological Layer | What needs to change in this case? |
| | How do we change it? |

| Structural Layer | What needs to change in this case? |
| | How do we change it? |

| Institutional Layer | What needs to change in this case? |
| | How do we change it? |

| Cultural Layer | What needs to change in this case? |
| | How do we change it? |

| Individual Layer | What needs to change in this case? |
| | How do we change it? |

Inequity in the Engineering Firm

In the space below, highlight the first (4) steps that you recommend the firm makes to get rid of the potential inequity.

Steps:

①

②

③

④

FINAL PROJECT: CREATE AN INFOGRAPHIC

Project: Create an Infographic
Time: 1 hour
Delivery: You will work independently on this project to create your own infographic

INSTRUCTIONS:

Based on what you have learned in this book, you will be creating an infographic that can be used to share with others. There are only a few requirements. First, it should be a digital resource, contain key concepts on what we covered in the course, and include some personal thoughts and ideas. Secondly, you will cite at least two credible sources mentioned in the book, or others you may have found in your own research. HINT: You might want to include your personal definitions of each of the five layers on the infographic.

As a bonus, you can include a second page to your infographic to educate and inform others on topics covered in the book or concepts that really resonated with you. Again, this is "your" infographic and you should be creative with it. You might choose to include elements of a personal story or maybe some other ideas.

When completed, please feel free to upload it on our website. There is a section on the website called "Post Infographics" where you can post your work for others to see. This is not a requirement. Have fun with it!

*Please refer to the Appendix for the short lesson on **Creating a Simple Infographic**

www.questversity.com

Conclusion

We have come to the end of this book, but this is certainly not the end of our journey to make our world a better place for all of us. There is nothing we can do to change our past. It is my hope that the activities that we covered in this book have helped you develop a better sense of what racism is so that you can think of ways to disrupt it when we see it operating. Viewing racism as a layered system helps to frame it and examine it through a critical lens. Hopefully the activities were engaging and got you to think about how your life might be impacted by racism or other forms of inequity. Through the many lives and voices from our past and present, there are many wonderful examples of people from all walks of life who have made significant progress in dismantling racism. Remember, becoming Antiracist requires "action". A best practice for engaging in tough conversations with disempowered groups is using the TREC Method. This ensures that we are putting careful *thought* into the problem, agreeing to *respect* those involved, showing *empathy*, and demonstrating *compassion*. I recommend that you use the strategies highlighted in this book. Let's continue to do the work that will make future generations proud of our efforts and enjoy the fruits of our labor.

Please visit our website for additional book updates and resources. I encourage you to use what you learned in this book and take a look at the other source materials noted as you build your toolbelt for addressing inequities. This will ensure you have the right resources on your journey to *Becoming Antiracist.*

Appendix

Short Lesson on Creating an Infographic

An infographic is a visual representation that consists of images, charts, graphs, and a little text. They are excellent ways to convey information, educate, and inform. In today's world, filled with rich social media embedded with video, images, and colorful graphics, it's important that we get the attention of our intended viewers.

There are a lot of tools out there to create infographics. I chose to use Canva because it's a free online tool and has a lot of cool features. The features that we need to create a basic infographic are available in the free plan. You can create the infographic online using one of the many pre-built templates and download it to one of the common file types such as JPG, PNG, and PDF. This is perfect for what you need to do in this project.

Let's get started!!!

Step 1: Enter www.canva.com into your browser's address bar. You can create a new account or log in using your email account.

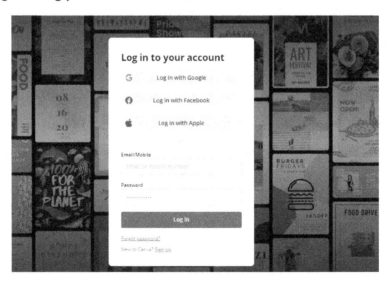

Step 2: Type "Infographic" into the search bar and select one of the design templates.

Step 3: Edit the text and graphics. You can change color schemes, upload your own images, and a variety of other things to make your graphic look the way you want

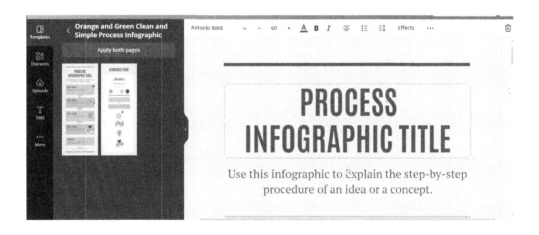

Step 4: After you have designed your infographic, you can now download it and share with others. Click the Download option at the top-right of the screen.

That's it!

Bibliography

Alexander, Michelle, *The New Jim Crow*. New York: New Press.

Allen, Theodore. *The Invention of the White Race, vol. 1, Racial Oppression and Social Control,* New York: Verso, 2012.

Anderson, Claud. *Powernomics: The National Plan to Empower Black America.* Maryland: PowerNomics Corporation, 2001.

Baradaran, Mehrsa "A Bad Check for Black America," Boston Review, August 8, 2018, https://www.bostonreview.net/class-inequality-race/mehrsa-baradaran-bad-check-black-america.

Battalora, Jacqueline. *Birth of a White Nation*. Houston, TX: Strategic Book Publishing, 2013.

Beazley, Raymond. "Prince Henry of Portugal and the African Crusade of the Fifteenth Century." *The American Historical Review* 16, no. 1 (1910): 11-23. Accessed August 21, 2021. doi:10.2307/1834305.

Blackmon, Douglas. *Slavery by Another Name*. New York: Anchor, 2008.

Browne, Harry. "N***** Love a Watermelon, HA! HA! Ha! Lyrics." Accessed September 22, 2021,https://tinyurl.com/rwfr4u6p

Coates, Ta-Nehisi. *Between the World and Me*. New York: One World, 2015.

Davenport, Frances. *European Treaties Bearing on the History of the United States and its Dependencies Vol. 1*. Washington, D.C.: Carnegie Institution of Washington, 1917.

Degruy, Joy. *Post Traumatic Slavery Syndrome: America's Legacy of Enduring Injury and Healing*. Joy DeGruy, 2017.

Dettling, Lisa. "Recent Trends in Wealth-Holding by Race and Ethnicity: Evidence from the Survey of Consumer Finances," The Fed - Recent Trends in Wealth-Holding by Race and Ethnicity: Evidence from the Survey of Consumer Finances, accessed August 22, 2021, https://doi.org/10.17016/2380-7172.2083.

DiAngelo, Robin. *White Fragility*. Boston, MA: Beacon Press, 2018.

Elattar, Hosam. "Black Student Union Demands Change After Fraternity's Racial Slur." Accessed October 22, 2019, https://dailytitan.com/news/campus/black-student-union-demands-change-after-fraternity-s-racial-slur/article_e212a9c7-c8f9-5908-baa2-39c9cb6cb0d6.html.

ElBoghdady, Dina. "FHA Needs $1.7 Billion Taxpayer Subsidy." Accessed September 27, 2013. https://www.washingtonpost.com/business/economy/fha-needs-17-billion-taxpayer-subsidy/2013/09/27/dd70ef90-276b-11e3-b3e9-d97fb087acd6_story.html.

Facing Hostory. "Inventing Black and White." Accessed on June 17,2021 from https://www.facinghistory.org/holocaust-and-human-behavior/chapter-2/inventing-black-and-white.

Federal Housing Authority. "Federal Housing Administration." Accessed August 22, 2021, https://www.hud.gov/program_offices/housing/fhahistory.

Fredrickson, George. *Racism: A Short History*. New Jersey: Princeton University Press, 2002.

Gutmann, Myron. "The Origins of the Thirty Years' War." Accessed August 20, 2021, https://www.jstor.org/stable/204823.

Haller, John. *Outcasts from Evolution: Scientific Attitudes of Racial Inferiority, 1859-1900*. Illinois: Southern Illinois University Press, 1971.

Hanslanger, Sally. *Resisting Reality*. New York: Oxford University Press, 2012.

Isaacs, Julia. "Economic Mobility of Black and White Families." Accessed July 28, 2016), https://www.brookings.edu/research/economic-mobility-of-black-and-white-families/.

Johnson, Theodore. "Recall That Ice Cream Truck Song? We Have Unpleasant News for You." Accessed May 11, 2014. https://www.npr.org/sections/codeswitch/2014/05/11/310708342/recall-that-ice-cream-truck-song-we-have-unpleasant-news-for-you.

Kendi, Ibram. *How to be an Antiracist*. New York: Random House, 2019.

Latin American Studies. "Wessell Webling, His Indenture (1622)." Accessed September 21, 2021. https://www.latinamericanstudies.org/united-states/indentured-contract.htm.

Library of Congress. "Interview with Fountain Hughes, Baltimore, Maryland, June 11, 1949." Accessed August 23, 2021, https://www.loc.gov/item/afc1950037_afs09990a/.

Library of Congress. "Germantown Friends' Protest against Slavery 1688." Accessed September 30, 2021. https://www.loc.gov/resource/rbpe.14000200/?st=text.

Lipsitz, George. *The Possessive Investment in Whiteness*. Philadelphia: Temple University Press, 2006.

Mancini, Matthew. *One Dies, Get Another: Convict Leasing in the American South, 1866-1928*. South Carolina: University of South Carolina Press, 1996.

McMillan, DuBois. *The World's Easiest Mini-Book on Improving your Memory Using Memory Palaces*. Los Angeles: QuestVersity, 2021.

Monroe, Ann. "Education, Society, & the K-12 Learner." Accessed August 20, 2021. https://courses.lumenlearning.com/teachereducationx92x1/chapter/piagets-theory-of-cognitive-development/.

Murdock, Jason."Humans Have More Than 6,000 Thoughts per Day, Psychologists Discover." Accessed July 15, 2020. https://www.newsweek.com/humans-6000-thoughts-every-day-1517963.

NAACP. "Criminal Justice Fact Sheet." Accessed May 24, 2021. https://www.naacp.org/criminal-justice-fact-sheet/.

NAACP. "The Origins of Modern Day Policing." Accessed May 9, 2021. https://naacp.org/find-resources/history-explained/origins-modern-day-policing.

National Constitution Center. "The 13th Amendment of the U.S. Constitution." Accessed August 22, 2021, https://constitutioncenter.org/interactive-constitution/amendment/amendment-xiii.

Oregon Coalition Against Domestic & Sexual Violence. "Working Definition of Allyship." Accessed August 1, 2021. https://www.ocadsv.org/sites/default/files/resource_pub/allyshipdefinition_handout.pdf

Parks, Gregory. "N*****: A Critical Race Realist Analysis of the N-Word within Hate Crimes Law." Accessed April 24, 2020 https://scholarlycommons.law.northwestern.edu/cgi/viewcontent.cgi?article=7306&context=jclc.

Perkinson, Robert. *Tough Texas: The Rise of America's Prison Empire*. New York: Metropolitan Books, 2010.

Roberts, Dorothy. *Fatal Invention: How Science, Politics, and Big Business Re-Create Race in the Twenty-First Century*. New York: The New Press, 2011.

Rolfe, John. "Twenty and Odd Negroes'; an Excerpt from a Letter from John Rolfe to Sir Edwin Sandys (1619/1620)." Accessed August 20, 2021, https://encyclopediavirginia.org/entries/twenty-and-odd-negroes-an-excerpt-from-a-letter-from-john-rolfe-to-sir-edwin-sandys-1619-1620/.

Rothstein, Richard. *The Color of Law*. New York: Liveright, 2017.

Saunders, A.C. DE C.M. *A Social History of Black Slaves and Freedmen in Portugal 1441-1555*. New York: Cambridge University Press, 1982.

Sharkey, Patrick. *Stuck in Place*. Chicago: University of Chicago Press, 2013

Shelby, Tommie. "Ideology, Racism, and Critical Social Theory," The Philosophical Forum Vol XXXIV, no. 2(2003).

Slavery and Remembrance." Middle Passage." Accessed August 21, 2021. http://slaveryandremembrance.org/articles/article/?id=A0032.

Smithsonian Magazine. "The Massacre of Black Sharecroppers That Led the Supreme Court to Curb the Racial Disparities of the Justice System." Accessed August 2, 2018. https://www.smithsonianmag.com/history/death-hundreds-elaine-massacre-led-supreme-court-take-major-step-toward-equal-justice-african-americans-180969863/.

Woodson, Cornell. "Developing our Ally Identity." Accessed August 16, 2021. https://cpb-us-e1.wpmucdn.com/blogs.cornell.edu/dist/3/6098/files/2016/01/ally-identity-okl2qw.pdf

Zurara, Gomes. *The Chronicle of the Discovery and Conquest of Guinea* New York: Cambridge University Press, 2010.

Made in the USA
Coppell, TX
24 November 2021